KARL KNUTSEN

Wild Plants You Can Eat

A GUIDE TO IDENTIFICATION AND PREPARATION

DOLPHIN BOOKS
Doubleday & Company, Inc., Garden City, New York
1975

Library of Congress Cataloging in Publication Data
Knutsen, Karl.
Wild plants you can eat.
Bibliography: p. 94
1. Plants, Edible—United States.   2. Cookery (Wild
foods)   I. Title.
QK98.5.U6K6   641.3′03
ISBN 0-385-09724-7
Library of Congress Catalog Card Number 74–12729

Dolphin Books Original Edition: 1975

ACKNOWLEDGMENTS

I would like to thank Sherry Moe for the countless hours expended and her persistence in doing the necessary research in order to make this book a reality.

I would also like to thank naturalist Tom Smith and Pat Koontz for their help and encouragement in getting me started.

And, I want to express my gratitude to the countless other people—botanists, librarians, naturalists, and friends —for their most valuable assistance.

Preface

Welcome to an adventure full of enjoyable new taste treats.

This book was not written as a text for botany students. It is intended to be a layman's guide to the tasty wild plants common to most of the United States. The one concession I have made is including the Latin name of each plant for the benefit of those who may be interested in further research. Even if you have no prior knowledge of plant life, this book will tell you where to look for a particular plant, how to properly identify it, how to harvest, prepare, and cook the edible parts for some really good eating. Realizing that taste is a matter of personal opinion, we acknowledge that you may like some of the foods our experimental group found tasty or interesting, and you may downright dislike others.

To be honest with you, it wasn't the spirit of adventure that prompted me to try my first wild plant food. Up to that point in my life, I had developed the reputation of being a finicky, rather fussy eater and experimenting with new foods was not my bag. My introduction was a result of trying to avoid the embarrassment of being the only one in a culinary clique to refuse elderberry fritters. Fortunately, this first experience turned out to be a very pleasant one.

With one successful experiment building up my confidence in wild plants as edible, I next tried a raw stalk of freshly cut cattail. I found the cattail had a unique though somewhat bland flavor of its own. To me, it was okay but not exciting.

6

The excitement was not long in coming. Tom Smith, a naturalist, really sold me on adding wild plant foods to my diet when he invited me to a breakfast at his home. While Tom cooked the pancakes, his wife, Billy Jo, set the table with what appeared to me to be bottles of wine but what were actually five different types of homemade syrup; elderberry, blackberry, wild strawberry, a combination of these, and rose hip. Domestic blueberry and strawberry syrups were familiar to me, but the taste of these wild syrups was totally new and different—a wonderfully delicious flavor. Having started with the elderberry, my inclination was to avoid the rose hip syrup because of its slight tomato aroma, not exactly what I would consider to be palatable with pancakes. However, the praising comments of other guests encouraged me to try the rose hip syrup and I discovered nectar from heaven. Nutritionists tell us that rose hip is loaded with vitamin C. I say: "Who cares! With such a taste, who needs the vitamins?"

OK, so wild plants can be tasty and loaded with vitamins. Isn't it too much trouble to find them and prepare them? Possibly . . . but only if you find it difficult to go to the market to buy vegetables and prepare them for eating. The typist who worked with me on the original manuscript asked "Where do you find this stuff?" To prove how easy it was, we went out into the back yard of her home in a suburban Minneapolis neighborhood. Within approximately twenty feet of her side door, we found lamb's-quarters, purslane, sheep sorrel, and green amaranth in enough abundance to add to daily salads or meals for their family of four for the rest of the summer and into early fall. She was flabbergasted. I hope you are as pleasantly surprised at how easy it is. Although many wild plants can be found in vacant city lots, city dwellers with no back yards may have to confine wild plant food gathering to walks in the country. For obvious reasons, I recommend careful washing of plants gathered in parks and vacant lots. Look, stoop, and pick . . . tasty, exciting foods are waiting for you, some so high that you don't even have to stoop. Look in your front yard, your back yard, down your garden path, in the woods where you camped last year. In fact, just about any place where there is soil, you are apt to find some tasty wild plant food.

Some soils are better suited to a particular plant than another type soil might be. If you look for a cattail in sandy soil that has been dry for a long time, you are not likely to find any. However, if you look for cattail in low marshy soils, you may find acres of them. Use this book as a guide in becoming familiar with the habitats of many wild plants. Check the *Where to Find* section to learn the type of soil and area where you will most likely find your chosen plant. Being able to find and identify any given plant will soon become second nature to you.

Where the information was available, I have tried to include the vitamin content on all the wild plants listed in this book. One should keep in mind that the vitamin contents of any food depends on many variables, such as the soil condition, rain or lack of it, time picked, how handled, how stored, how eaten (raw or cooked), and method of cooking. All references to vitamin contents were included only as a guide.

The color photos in this book will help eliminate the need for a lot of study and make it easier to identify each of the plants listed herein. To make it more enjoyable reading, I have purposely omitted botanical terms.

By reading *Where to Find*, looking at the photographs, and reading the descriptions, you can soon be enjoying a great variety of TASTY WILD PLANTS.

8

Contents

Arrowhead

Sagittaria: And related species.

Other Common Names: Arrowleaf, swamp potato, tule potato, duck potato, swan potato, wapatoo, katniss.

Picture Reference Numbers: 1, 14

Where to Find: Arrowhead is found in fresh or brackish shallow water of ponds, swamps, or streams with rich mud bottoms. You may find two or three plants grouped together or hundreds or thousands.

Identifying Characteristics: True to its name, the leaves of this aquatic plant are shaped like arrowheads and vary from four to twelve inches in length. They are three-lobed and rise directly from the root on long leafstalks. The flowers usually appear in groups of three on a tall single stalk which often extends above the top of the leaves. The fragile white flowers have three petals and later turn to flat seeds. The roots are fine and fibrous, enlarging in areas to form tubers. The tubers are pure white with a smooth texture.

Edible Parts: Tubers.

When to Harvest: Tubers: From late summer or early fall to spring when the plant leaf is usually brown and shriveled.

How to Harvest: The Indians gathered the tubers by wading through the water and digging them up with their toes. However, you can dig around the mud with a rake or hoe; the tubers will break free from the roots and float to the surface. They vary in size from that of a pea to two inches in diameter.

How to Prepare and Cook: Wash, scrape, and peel the tubers as thinly as possible. They can be eaten raw, though cooked the same way as potatoes—baked, boiled, roasted, or fried—they taste better. They are particularly tasty when roasted.

How to Store: Store the tubers in a cool, dry, dark place. They will keep about as long as potatoes stored in this manner. The tubers can also be dried in the sun or in a very slow oven—about 175° F. Once dried, they grind easily into a flour. Use a hand flour mill, if available. You can also use a kitchen blender or rub the tubers between two flat rocks.

RECIPES TO TRY

Arrowhead Tubers with Mint Leaves
Scrape and clean 1½ pounds of arrowhead tubers. Boil in salted water until tender, approximately 20 to 30 minutes. Peel tubers and pour ¼ cup of melted butter over them. Season with salt and pepper; then roll the tubers in ⅓ cup finely chopped mint leaves and serve. Serves 4.

Scalloped Arrowhead Tubers

Clean and scrape 1½ pounds arrowhead tubers. Slice them to ¼ inch thick and place one layer of sliced tubers in a greased baking dish. Sprinkle the layer with salt, pepper, flour, and grated cheese. Dot with butter, then repeat with another layer of sliced tubers until there are three layers. Slowly add milk until it can be seen between the sliced tubers. Cover and bake in a 350° F. oven approximately 30 minutes or until the tubers are tender when pierced with a fork. Remove the cover the last 15 minutes of baking to brown the top. Serves 4.

Glazed Arrowhead Tubers

Clean and scrape 1 to 2 pounds medium-sized arrowhead tubers. Boil the tubers in salted water until soft, about 25 minutes. Peel the boiled tubers as thinly as possible. Dip each tuber in melted butter. Then sprinkle well with salt, paprika, and brown sugar. Place in a heavy skillet over low heat and cook until the tubers are well glazed. Baste from time to time with more melted butter. Serves 3 to 5.

Arrowhead Salad

Boil and peel 1 quart of arrowhead tubers. Mix the cooled, sliced tubers with 5 or 6 hard-cooked eggs, chopped onions, to taste, and pickles. Add mayonnaise, ½ teaspoon prepared mustard, and salt and pepper to taste. Top with paprika and serve cold. Serves 6 to 9.

Arrowhead Hash

Scrape and clean 1½ pounds arrowhead tubers. Peel

13

them as thinly as possible and cook in salted water for 15 minutes. Drain, cool, and dice tubers into ¼-inch cubes. To the chopped tubers, add 1 cup chopped, cooked corned beef, 1 onion, diced, ¾ teaspoon salt, ⅛ teaspoon pepper, and ⅓ cup milk. Melt 3 tablespoons of butter in a skillet and add the hash, spreading it evenly over the bottom. Cook slowly until brown on the bottom and fold over as you would an omelet. Serves 4.

Black Cherry and Chokecherry

Prunus serotina—Prunus virginiana

Other Common Names: Black cherry is also known as rum cherry.

Picture Reference Numbers: 2, 15

Where to Find: Black cherry is found along fences and roadsides; chokecherry is found on the border of woods, roadsides, swamps, and thickets.

Identifying Characteristics: Black cherry is a large forest tree that can reach up to 100 feet in height. It begins fruiting at about 15 feet. On mature trees, the bark on the trunk is dark and reddish on the branches. The leaves are thick and shiny; oblong to lance-shaped with a prominent midrib and blunt teeth along the edges. The flowers are white; the red fruit turns to a purplish black when ripe. They are borne on long racemes that look like bunches of grapes.

Chokecherry is similar, but smaller; growing to a height of about 20 feet. The leaves are thinner, more oval, and pointed with sharp, fine teeth along the edges. When ripe, the fruit is dark red or crimson and borne on shorter clusters.

Edible Parts: Fruit.

When to Harvest: Fruit: August or September.

How to Harvest: Pick berries when ripe.

How to Prepare and Cook: Black cherries can be eaten fresh, but chokecherries, true to their name, are much too bitter to be eaten raw. However, cooking removes the astringency and both species make good jellies and sauces. The fruit makes an especially good jelly when mixed with apple. To make syrup, put a quart of the fruit in a saucepan and add a few tablespoons of water to help it start boiling. Mash the fruit while boiling. Strain out the juice and boil two parts juice to one part sugar for about 5 to 10 minutes. A good test at the end of 5 minutes is to take ½ teaspoon of the liquid, cool rapidly by placing the bottom of the spoon in cold water, and if the liquid is then the syrupy consistency desired, your syrup, when cooled, is ready. Use the syrup on pancakes and waffles, or for a jelly base. Chill the syrup and add water for a cold fruit soup or beverage. Yields approximately 3 pints.

Caution: The pits of the fruit, and the leaves, contain toxic levels of hydrocyanic acid and cyanide. The toxicity is destroyed by cooking. Raw pits *should never* be eaten!

How to Store: The fruit can be dried to store. Wash the pitted fruit and spread on a screen or stretched cloth under direct sunlight. Cover the fruit with cheesecloth to keep the flies away. Turn the fruit occasionally, and bring indoors at night. The drying process usually takes several days. The fruit can also be dried on trays in a very slow oven, about 175° F. Once the fruit is dried, seal in jars and store. To use the dried fruit, eat as is or soak in cold water for several hours and use them the same way you would the fresh fruit.

Another method for storing this fruit is freezing. Make a syrup by boiling equal amounts of sugar and water together until the sugar dissolves. Let the syrup cool and pour over cherries that have been packed in canning jars. Seal the jars and freeze immediately. The frozen fruit can be used the same way as fresh fruit.

RECIPES TO TRY

Brandied Black Cherries

Boil together 5 cups of sugar and 2 cups of water for 10 minutes or until the syrup is transparent. Pour the syrup over 5 pounds of black cherries (washed, pitted), and let stand overnight. The next day, boil the mixture for several minutes. Remove the cherries and put in hot, sterilized glass jars, leaving room at the top. Boil the syrup until thick, and add 1 pint of commercial brandy. Pour the mixture over the cherries and seal. You will have enough for 20 to 30 future servings.

Candied Black Cherries

Boil 1 pound of sugar in 1 cup of water until the sugar spins a thread. Test this by dipping your forefinger into a rapidly cooled teaspoon of the syrup and applying it to your thumb. When you pull the thumb and forefinger apart, a fine thread should appear. Once the syrup has reached this stage, add 1 pound of washed, pitted black cherries. Let the syrup and the cherries come to a boil and cool. Remove the cherries from the syrup with a perforated spoon to a platter. Boil the syrup for 5 minutes, then pour over the cherries. Let the cherries dry and store in glass jars. Serves 5 to 8.

RECIPES TO TRY

Chokecherry Pudding

Pour 1 quart of hot, scalded milk over 2 cups of bread crumbs. Add a little salt. Mix in 3 tablespoons of butter, 4 slightly beaten eggs, and 1½ cups of sugar. Then, add 1 quart of washed, pitted chokecherries. Pour into a baking dish and bake in a 350° F. oven until well set. Serves 8.

Cold Chokecherry Soup

Cook 2 tablespoons tapioca in 1 cup of boiling water until tender. Add more water, if necessary. Boil together 1 quart of pitted cherries, 1 quart of water, ½ cup of sugar, 3 inches of cinnamon stick, and the juice of 1 lemon. Let boil for 15 minutes. Add the cooked tapioca. Bring it to a boil and pour very gradually over 2 well-beaten egg yolks. Serve cold. Serves 6 to 9.

Wild Cherry or Chokecherry Jelly with Apple

Stem and wash fruit. You need not remove all the small green stems. Use equal parts of fruit and water. Boil gently until fruit is pulpy. Strain through a jelly bag overnight.

17

Measure and add tart apple juice in equal parts. Use ¾ cup sugar for each cup of juice. Boil gently until 2 drops run together and form a sheet on a spoon. Skim and pour into hot glasses or small jars. Seal with paraffin or canning jar lids.

Wild Cherry or Chokecherry Jelly with Pectin
Stem and wash fruit. You need not remove all the small green stems. Use equal parts of fruit and water. Boil gently until fruit is pulpy. Strain through a jelly bag overnight.
Pour 3 cups of the juice into a large kettle. Add 6½ cups of sugar and stir to mix. Place over high heat. Bring to a boil, stirring constantly. Stir in 1 (6-ounce) bottle of commercial liquid pectin.
Bring to a rolling boil and boil rapidly for 1 minute, stirring constantly. Remove from heat. Stir and skim for 5 minutes. Add ¼ teaspoon of almond extract, if desired, and pour into hot glasses or small jars. Seal with paraffin or canning jar lids. Makes about 9 half-pints.

Blue-berried Elder

Sambucus canadensis, Sambucus melanocarpa

Other Common Names: Elder, elderberry.

Picture Reference Numbers: 3, 4, 16

Where to Find: Blue-berried elder can be found in damp places such as the rich moist soil of stream banks, ditches, woods, and along fences and roadsides. *Sambu-*

cus canadensis is found mostly in the East and *Sambucus melanocarpa* in the West.

Identifying Characteristics: Blue-berried elder grow on shrubs that range from 5 to 12 feet high, larger plants are found in the South. The two species are very similar. The bark on the young stems is greenish, that on older branches is grayish brown. The leaves are composed of from 5 to 11 leaflets arranged along a central stalk. The leaflets are elliptical to lance-shaped and have pointed tips with serrated edges. The small, white, star-shaped flowers bloom in June in clusters that are flat and measure up to 8 inches across. In the fall, the flowers mature to clusters of round waxy berries that are blue, purple, or black when ripe.

Caution: The red-berried elder (*Sambucus racemosa* and other species) is very similar but is not edible. *Red*-berried elder has *rounded* flower clusters unlike the flat clusters of the edible *blue*-berried elder described above. The inedible red-berried elder plant blooms earlier in the season than its edible relative. The fruit of the *blue*-berried elder turns blue, purple, or black when ripe while the fruit of *red*-berried elder remains red. The *red*-berries are very bitter and are considered toxic. The leaves, shoots, bark, twigs, and roots of all varieties of red-berried elder are also toxic.

Edible Parts: Flowers and berries.

When to Harvest:
   Flowers: June or July.
   Berries: August or early September.

How to Harvest:

Flowers: The clusters of blossoms are called elder blow. Gather the entire *flat* cluster from the blue-berried elder before the blossoms are fully opened. Remember, they bloom *after* the rounded clusters of the red-berried elder.

Berries: Elder berries are one of the easiest to harvest as the entire cluster is easily broken from the stem; the berries can then easily be pulled off into a container. Harvest the berries when they are fully ripe—blue, purple, or black in color.

How to Prepare and Cook:

Flowers: Wash the flowers by dipping the cluster into a solution made of 1 teaspoon salt per quart of water. Then rinse them in fresh water. This process rids any of the tiny bugs that tend to hide in the blossom. Of course if you want the extra protein the bugs provide you can omit this process.

After washing dip the entire cluster into a batter and fry as fritters (see recipes for batter). You can also remove the stems from the cluster and add the individual blossoms to pancakes, muffins, and scrambled eggs.

The blossoms are also used for making wine and tea. Fully expanded blossoms steeped for a tea are reportedly good for colds and high blood pressure.

Berries: Elder berries aren't very palatable eaten raw, but are delicious cooked or dried. The fresh fruit can be added to pancakes, muffins, and pie fillings, although I recommend they be dried first.

It is easy to make a syrup from the berries that is good on pancakes, etc. or for a jelly base. The fruit is very juicy, so there is no need to add any water while boiling. Put the washed berries in a saucepan, mash them slightly, and boil for a few minutes. Strain the juice out and return it to the saucepan. Add one part sugar to two parts juice and boil these together with a little lemon juice. Store the syrup in glass jars in the refrigerator.

The use of elder berries in making wine is well known, but a good nonalcoholic beverage can also be made from the fruit. Extract the juice from the berries and mix one part berry juice with three parts sumac or lemon juice. Sweeten to taste with honey or sugar, bring to a boil, and pour into sterilized jars if canned.

How to Store: Dry the berries by spreading washed berries on a screen or stretched cloth outdoors in direct sunlight. Cover with cheesecloth to keep off the flies, turn occasionally, and bring them in at night. It usually takes several days to dry the fruit. You can also dry them in the oven, by placing them on racks in a very slow oven —about 175° F. Turn occasionally. The dried fruit can then be placed in jars or plastic bags for storage.

Dried berries can be used as the fruit ingredient in pemmican, a trail food originated by the Indians. Pemmican is made from dried meat, fat, and dried berries which have been formed into small, flat cakes. Pemmican keeps for a long time without refrigeration and can be eaten raw, boiled, or fried.

Additional Information: Blue-berried elder is rich in vitamins A and C, and also high in calcium, iron, and potassium. It is richer in vitamin C than citrus fruits or tomatoes.

21

RECIPES TO TRY

Elderberry Pie

For the piecrust, sift together 2 cups of flour and ¾ teaspoon salt. Cut in ⅔ cup of shortening with a knife or pastry blender. Add 4 to 6 tablespoons of cold water a little at a time, until the mixture holds together. Divide the dough in half and roll out on a floured board. Line a 9-inch piepan. Or, follow your favorite two-crust pie recipe.

Fill the unbaked piecrust with 2½ cups of washed berries, stems removed. Mix together ½ cup sugar, ⅛ teaspoon salt, 2 tablespoons of flour, and sprinkle over the berries. Add 3 tablespoons lemon juice. Cover with top crust. Bake in a 450° F. oven for 10 minutes. Lower the oven to 350° and bake for 30 minutes more. Serves 6.

Elderberry Jelly

Crush 3 pounds of washed berries, stems removed, in a saucepan and simmer for 15 minutes. Squeeze through a jelly bag and return the juice to a saucepan. Add the juice of 1 lemon and 1 (1¾-ounce) package of commercial pectin. Bring to a boil and then boil for 1 minute, stirring constantly. Add 5 cups sugar and boil for 1 minute more. Pour into sterilized jars and seal. Yields 2½ pints.

Elder Blossom Fritters

Beat together 2 egg yolks, ⅓ cup of water, and ⅓ cup evaporated milk. Then, beat in 1 tablespoon lemon juice and 1 tablespoon butter. Sift together 1 cup of flour, ¼ teaspoon salt, and 2 tablespoons of sugar and blend with egg yolk mixture. Then, beat 2 egg whites with ⅛ teaspoon salt until stiff. Add to the rest of the batter.

Dip the clusters of washed blue-berried elder blossoms (still on the stems) in the batter and fry in deep fat until they are a delicate golden brown. Sprinkle with a little lemon juice and confectioners' sugar. Serve 2 clusters per person.

Elder Blossom Pancakes

Sift together ¾ cup of flour, ½ teaspoon salt, 1 teaspoon baking powder, and 2 tablespoons powdered sugar. Beat 2 eggs and add ⅔ cup milk, ⅓ cup water, and ½ teaspoon vanilla. Add ½ cup of washed blue-berried elder blossoms with the stems removed, and combine with the dry ingredients. Cook the batter in a greased skillet as you would pancakes. Serves 3 to 4.

Cattail

Typhia latifolia

Other Common Names: Rushes, Cossack asparagus, cat-o'-nine-tails, flags, swamp bulrush, reed mace.

Picture Reference Numbers: 5, 6, 17

Where to Find: Cattails are found in shallow water along streams and marshes, and at the margins of ponds and lakes.

Identifying Characteristics: Cattail grows anywhere from 3 to 12 feet high at maturity. Its most prominent feature is the cigar-shaped flower spike found at the top of a long stalk. The stalk is surrounded and tightly sheathed at the base by long pale green, tape-like leaves. In the spring, the flower spike is green with a tightly sheathed husk. As it breaks through the husk, it starts forming yellow pollen and then turns brown. In the fall it goes to seed turning gray and fluffy. Some of the cottony mass of seeds will cling to the spike throughout the winter. The roots are ropelike and branch frequently.

Edible Parts: Flowerhead, shoots and stems, roots.

When to Harvest:
Flowerhead: Spring and summer.
Shoots and Stems: Spring and summer.
Roots: Year round.

How to Harvest:
Flowerhead: In the spring, harvest the green immature spikes. They are most tender just as the husks are about to break open; be sure to get them before they start turning brown. Cattails reach maturity over a six-week period, so you can still find the green cobs through part of summer. In the spring and summer, gather the loose yellow pollen formed on slightly older spikes by cutting the spikes and rubbing them through your hand over a container.
Shoots and Stems: When the leaves are 1 to 2 feet high, the shoot can be harvested by pulling on the cluster of leaves which will cause the shoot to come free from the roots; or, cut the stem just below the water line.
Caution: Be careful not to confuse the young shoots

24

. The edible tubers of arrowhead are eady for harvesting when the plant leaf s brown and shriveled—from late ummer or early fall to spring.

2. The fruit from the black cherry and chokecherry plants are borne in long clusters that look like bunches of grapes.

3. Elder blow is the name given to the flat cluster of blossoms of blue-berried elder.

4. Elder blossom fritters, sprinkled with confectioners' sugar.

5. #2 & #4 are the most suitable cattail flower heads for preparing and eating as you would corn-on-the-cob.

6. The cylindrical cattail shoots can be harvested by cutting the stem just below the water line.

7. Gather the young dandelion leaves early in the spring before the flower stem appears.

8. In the fall, the dock flowers are replaced with tiny, dark brown seeds which can be ground to make a flour similar to buckwheat.

9. The edible leaves from evening primrose should be gathered from the first-year plant. These are the long leaves that form a rosette which lies flat on the ground, not the small leaves that cover the flower stalk of the second-year plant.

10. To give an idea of the size of the gooseberry fruit, the plant is displayed against graph paper, the larger squares are 1 inch and the smaller ones, ¼ inch.

11. The flowers, which produce edible pollen for making flour, occur in spikelike clusters just below the tip of the stem on the great bulrush plant.

12. Harvest the young leaves from green amaranth plants that have not yet flowered—from spring to fall.

13. The greenish flowers of green amaranth appear late in summer and are borne at the top of the stem in long, panicled spikes.

with those of blue flag which are poisonous. Cattail shoots are perfectly cylindrical down to the base whereas blue flag shoots are flattened.

Roots: Dig up the roots together with the enlarged bulb-like areas at the ends that form next year's sprouts.

How to Prepare and Cook:

Flowerhead: The green spikes make a tasty cooked vegetable. Husk them and boil in salted water. They smell much like sweet corn while cooking and are eaten the same way—either on the cob or off. Generously butter the hot spikes as they are somewhat dry and granular.

The yellow pollen makes an excellent flour. It is already very fine and therefore does not need grinding. The taste is similar to that of buckwheat. The flour can be used alone, but is better when mixed with equal parts of wheat flour or other flours. The pollen adds a rich coloring and good taste to pancakes, muffins, breads, and cake.

Shoots and Stems: Peel away the leaves to expose the crisp inner white core. Cut away the bitter green parts. The core can be eaten raw in salads or cooked as you would asparagus. Throughout the summer, the inner core of the stem can be cut into segments and cooked as an ingredient in soups and stews.

Roots: The bulblike areas have a starchy core from fall to early spring. Peel, wash, and eat them raw or prepared and cooked like potatoes.

How to Store:

Flowerhead: To store the green spikes, boil them for a few minutes, package, and freeze. The yellow pollen can be stored in a container like flour.

Shoots and Stems: Blanch the stems by quickly dipping in boiling water, wrap in freezer paper or plastic bags, and freeze.

Roots: The roots of cattail make a highly nutritious flour. Peel the roots down to the white core which is about ½ inch in diameter. Dry this root core; pulverize and sift out the fibers. Or crush the white core in water, strain out the fibers, and allow the starchy material to settle to the bottom through several changes of water. Pour off the water and allow to dry.

Additional Information:

Flowerhead: Cattail pollen is a good source of protein and vitamin A.

Shoots and Stems: Not established.

Roots: Flour made from cattail roots is equal in nutritional value to any other flour. During the winter months, the roots are at their peak as a source of starch.

RECIPES TO TRY

Cattail Root Stew

Cut 2 pounds of stew meat into 1-inch pieces. Wash and peel 2 pounds of cattail roots and cut into ¼-inch slices. Slice 6 onions. In a 3-quart casserole dish, line the bottom with a layer of meat. Salt and pepper. Top with a layer of cattail roots and a layer of onions. Repeat until all the ingredients are used. Pour a small amount of water over the layers and cover. Cook in a slow oven (325° F.) for about 2 hours, or until the meat is tender. Serve hot. Serves 6 to 10.

Sunshine Pancakes

Sift together 1 cup cattail pollen, 1 cup wheat flour, 2 teaspoons baking powder, ½ teaspoon salt, and 2 tablespoons sugar.

Beat 2 eggs and stir in 1½ cups of milk and 2 tablespoons melted butter. Stir in the dry ingredients. Fry the batter in a skillet with melted butter as you would for pancakes. Serves 3 to 4.

Cattail Coffee Cake

Scrape and clean several cattail roots and dry them in a slow oven overnight. Skin the roots and remove the fibers. Put through a blender until fine and let the flour set overnight until completely dry.

Scald ½ cup of milk. Add ½ cup shortening, ½ cup sugar, and ½ teaspoon salt to the milk. Stir together until the sugar dissolves and cool until lukewarm. Dissolve 1 package of dry active yeast in ¼ cup of warm water. Combine with milk mixture. Stir in 1½ cups of cattail flour. Add 2 beaten eggs and stir well. Add 1½ to 2 cups more of the cattail flour; enough to make a soft dough. Knead the dough on a floured board until smooth and elastic. Put in a greased bowl and brush with butter. Cover and let rise in a warm place until dough doubles in bulk, approximately two hours.

On a floured board, roll the dough into a rectangle about 8 by 12 inches. Brush with butter and sprinkle with brown sugar and cinnamon. Roll up and shape into a ring on a greased cookie sheet. Pinch the ends. At 1 inch intervals, slice the ring part of the way through from the outside toward the center. Fan the slices and brush with butter. Cover and let rise until dough doubles in bulk, about 45 minutes.

Bake in a 375° F. oven for 25 to 30 minutes. Spread with

icing and sprinkle with chopped nuts while it is still warm. Serves 6 to 10.

Weed Bread

Heat 1 cup of cottage cheese to lukewarm. Dissolve 1 package of dry yeast in ¼ cup warm water. Add to cottage cheese. Then add 1 slightly beaten egg, 2 tablespoons grated onion, 1 tablespoon melted butter or margarine, 1 tablespoon sugar or honey, 1 tablespoon dill (or penny cress, oregano, sweet basil, or thyme), 1 teaspoon salt, ¼ teaspoon baking soda, and ⅛ to ¼ cup cattail pollen. Mix well, then stir in about 1½ cups of unbleached flour until mixture is somewhat stiff. Let rise for 1 hour. The bulk should be about double.

Turn onto lightly floured board. Knead an additional 1½ cups unbleached flour into the dough and shape into a round loaf before putting into a buttered 1½- to 2-quart casserole dish. Let rise about 1 hour. Bulk should once again double.

Bake 40 minutes in a preheated oven set at 350° F. Bread should be nicely browned and slightly crusty. Let cool 10 minutes before removing from dish. Remove bread from baking dish and lightly butter crust. Allow bread to cool completely before slicing.

Chufa

Cyperus esculentus

Other Common Names: Nutgrass, earth almond, ground almond.

Picture Reference Number: 18

Where to Find: Chufa is found in damp, sandy soil; and, less commonly, in cultivated soil.

Identifying Characteristics: The chufa plant stands about 2 feet high and has a triangular stem surrounded at its base by pale green, tape-like leaves that grow as high as the plant. The stem is topped by a cluster of 3 to 9 smaller leaves that curve up and around the flower clusters.

The flower clusters occur on many branches and are composed of many tiny golden brown flowers.

The roots of chufa appear as thin runners which grow horizontally from the base of the plant. At the ends of these runners are dark, round, wrinkled tubers, measuring about ¼ to ½ inch in diameter.

Edible Parts: Tubers.

When to Harvest: Tubers: Spring through fall.

How to Harvest: In loose, sandy soil, the tubers are found near the base of the plant and can be dug up easily. Do it carefully, as the runners bearing the tubers break easily.

How to Prepare and Cook: Chufa tubers have a sweet, nutty taste similar to almonds or filberts. They can be eaten alone, either fresh or boiled.

For a cold, refreshing drink, soak the tubers in cold water for two days. Then, smash or blend the tubers in a kitchen blender with fresh water and sugar. Strain, chill, and serve.

For a coffee substitute, roast the tubers until dark brown, grind, and brew as coffee.

How to Store: Thoroughly dry the tubers over a slow fire or in a slow oven. Once dried, chufa tubers grind into one of nature's best wild flours. The dried tubers will keep almost indefinitely.

RECIPES TO TRY

Chufa Muffins
Dry chufa tubers in a slow oven for several hours, leaving oven door slightly open to allow moisture to escape. When the tubers are thoroughly dried, grind small amounts at a time in blender until you have a fine flour.

Combine 1 cup of chufa flour with 1 cup wheat flour, ½ teaspoon salt, 4 teaspoons baking powder, and 2 tablespoons sugar. Mix 1 cup milk with 1 beaten egg and 3 tablespoons melted butter. Add the flour mixture and stir just until the flour is moistened; do not overstir. Pour into well-greased muffin tins and bake in a 450° F. oven for 15 to 20 minutes until done. Makes 10 to 12.

Chufa Soufflé

Beat 8 egg yolks with 1½ cups sugar until creamy. Add 2 teaspoons grated lemon rind, 2 cups grated chufa tubers, and ¼ cup bread crumbs.

Beat 8 egg whites with ⅛ teaspoon salt until stiff. Fold into the egg yolk and chufa mixture. Pour into a greased baking dish and set the dish in a pan of hot water. Bake in a 325° F. oven for 45 minutes or until it is firm. Top with whipped cream, before or after cutting, and serve either warm or cold. Serves 6.

Chufa Wafers

Dry chufa tubers in a slow oven for several hours, leaving oven door slightly open to allow moisture to escape. When the tubers are thoroughly dried, grind small amounts at a time in a kitchen blender until you have a fine flour.

Blend 1 cup sugar with 1 cup softened butter until creamy. Beat in 2 eggs. Add 1 teaspoon grated lemon rind, ⅛ teaspoon salt, and 2 cups chopped nuts. Stir in 1 cup chufa flour and 1 cup wheat flour. Chill the dough. On a floured board roll the dough to about ⅛ inch thickness and cut into any desired shapes. Brush tops of wafers with a mixture of 1 egg yolk and 2 tablespoons milk. Sprinkle with sugar and bake on greased cookie sheet in a 350° F. oven for 15 to 20 minutes.

Sugared Chufas

Soak 1 pound of chufa tubers in cold water for a couple of days, then drain and dry.

Boil 2 cups of sugar with ½ cup water until the syrup is thick and clear. Add the chufa tubers and stir until well coated. Lower heat and stir until syrup is dry. Remove the chufas. Add a small amount of water to the sugar remaining in the pan. If desired, you may add just a bit of cinnamon and red food coloring. Boil until the syrup becomes transparent. Add the sugared chufas and stir until well coated. Serves 6.

Dandelion

Taraxacum officinale

Other Common Names: None available.

Picture Reference Numbers: 7, 19

Where to Find: Dandelions are found in grassy open places such as fields, meadows, waste areas, and lawns.

Identifying Characteristics: Dandelions grow from 3 to 5 inches high with flower stems reaching up to 15 inches. The oblong leaves have irregular serrated edges and are narrow at their base to form a rosette at the top of a somewhat forked taproot. The flower heads occur on single hollow stems growing out of the center of the rosette of leaves. The green buds open up to a bright yellow flower head. These in turn mature into silky balls that release wind-borne seeds.

Edible Parts: Leaves, leaf crown, roots, and flowers.

When to Harvest:
    Leaves: Early spring.

Leaf Crowns: Spring and summer.
Roots: Year round.
Flowers: Early spring to summer.

How to Harvest:

Leaves: Gather the young leaves early in the spring before the flower stem appears.

Leaf Crown: Dig deep to the root and cut off the top of the root 2 or 3 inches below the ground. Collect the top of the root and the base part of the leaves that is white.

Roots: Dig up the taproots any time, though they are at their best in the early spring.

Flowers: Collect the young unopened buds in early spring. The tastiest ones are found close to the ground, hiding inside the rosette of leaves. Collect the bright yellow flowers later in the season.

How to Prepare and Cook:

Leaves: The very young leaves are good eaten raw in salads. The slightly older leaves can be cooked as a potherb. Boil in a small amount of salted water. The leaves get progressively bitter as they get older, and it may be necessary to change the cooking water at least once while preparing as a potherb.

Leaf Crowns: This blanched white part of the plant is not at all bitter and is considered a delicacy in many parts of the world. It can be eaten raw in salads or briefly cooked as a potherb.

Roots: To make a tasty cooked vegetable, peel the roots and cook in two changes of water with a pinch of bicarbonate of soda added to the first.

Flowers: The unopened buds can be eaten raw, but are especially good as a cooked vegetable when steamed in a small amount of salted water for several minutes. Fully opened flowers are used for making dandelion wine.

How to Store: The dandelion roots can be used to make a coffee substitute. Roast the washed, peeled roots before a slow fire or in a 300° F. oven until they are completely dry and dark brown throughout, about 4 hours. Then grind and brew like coffee. The dandelion brew is stronger than regular coffee, so use only 1 teaspoon per cup.

Additional Information:
Leaves: Dandelion greens are high in vitamins A, C, B, and calcium, phosphorous, and iron.
Flowers: The unopened buds provide vitamins A and C.

RECIPES TO TRY

Dandelion Salad
Wash and gently dry 2 quarts of young tender dandelion leaves. Arrange in a salad bowl and sprinkle with bits of crispy fried bacon. Set in the refrigerator.
For the dressing, melt ¼ cup of butter and ½ cup of light cream in a skillet over low heat. Beat together 2 eggs, 1 teaspoon salt, a little pepper and paprika, 1 tablespoon of sugar, and 4 tablespoons of vinegar. Blend this in with the melted butter and cream and heat slowly until the mixture becomes thick. Pour over the dandelion greens and stir well. Serves 4 to 6.

Creamed Dandelion
Thoroughly wash 2 quarts of young dandelion leaves. Steam the leaves until tender. Drain well. Chop the greens very finely.

Melt 3 tablespoons of butter in a skillet. Cook 1 tablespoon of finely chopped onion in the butter until tender. Stir in 2½ tablespoons of flour until well blended. Slowly add 1 cup of hot cream; stir constantly. When the sauce is smooth and boiling, add the chopped dandelion greens. Stir and cook over medium heat for 3 minutes or until well blended. Season with salt and pepper. If desired, sprinkle with nutmeg before serving. Serves 6 to 8.

Dock

Rumex crispus: And related species.

Other Common Names: Yellow dock, curled dock, narrow-leafed dock.

Picture Reference Numbers: 8, 20

Where to Find: Dock is found in fields, pastures, disturbed ground, waste areas, and sometimes in swamps, depending on the species. (It usually grows near stinging nettle. However, areas of the skin irritated by the nettle can be relieved by rubbing them with the juicy dock leaves.)

Identifying Characteristics: Dock grows from 1 to 3 feet high. Most of the leaves are found at the base of the plant. The leaves, smooth on both sides, are dark green and lance-shaped, with curly or wavy edges. Similar, but smaller leaves occur along the stem. The tiny, scaly green flowers appear in tightly packed whorls on the upper part of the stem. In the fall, the flowers are replaced with tiny, dark brown seeds. Each seed is surrounded by 3 papery, membranelike wings.

Edible Parts: Leaves and seeds.

When to Harvest:
  Leaves: Spring.
  Seeds: Fall to winter.

How to Harvest:
  Leaves: Collect young leaves in the spring before the plant has flowered. They lose little bulk in cooking, so small quantities are sufficient.
  Seeds: Collect seeds by pulling the stem through the palm of the hand over a container.

How to Prepare and Cook:
  Leaves: Dock leaves are too bitter to be eaten raw; but cooked, they make an excellent potherb. Rinse the leaves and boil for 3 to 4 minutes. If the taste is still too bitter, change the cooking water and boil a few more minutes. Season with a little vinegar. Dock leaves are good served with ham or bacon.
  Seeds: Break the husks free from the seeds by rubbing them through your hands. Winnow out the trash by pouring the seeds from one container to another in the wind, letting the air blow away the trash. The seeds can then be ground into a flour resembling buckwheat. Grind the seeds with a mortar and pestle, or in a kitchen blender, or in a hand flour mill.

How to Store: Must be used immediately.

Additional Information: Dock greens are extremely high

in vitamin A content; and also rich in vitamin C, calcium, iron, and potassium.

Caution: Since dock leaves are very rich in vitamin A, and large doses of vitamin A are considered toxic, dock should be used only moderately.

RECIPES TO TRY

Creamed Dock

Steam and chop 2 cups of dock greens. Melt 1 tablespoon of butter in a saucepan over low heat and blend in 1 tablespoon flour. Add the 2 cups of greens and ½ cup milk. Heat slowly until mixture thickens slightly, stirring constantly. Salt and pepper to taste. Serves 4 to 6.

Clam Soup with Dock

Wash and shred 2 cups of young dock leaves. Lightly sauté 1 large onion, chopped, in 3 tablespoons of butter. Add the dock leaves and stir for 1 minute. Stir in 2 cups of cleaned clams and 2 cups of milk. Bring to a low boil and season with pepper. Serves 4 to 6.

Evening Primrose

Oenothera biennis

Other Common Names: German rampion, scurvish, night willow herb.

Picture Reference Numbers: 9, 21

Where to Find: Evening primrose can be found in dry open soil of waste areas, fields, and roadsides.

Identifying Characteristics: Evening primrose is a biennial plant. In the first year, the lance-shaped leaves that are 4 to 8 inches long form a rosette that lies flat on the ground. The leaves are smooth-edged, sometimes slightly curly with white or reddish prominent midribs. The rosette of leaves is attached to the top of a stout, fleshy, branched taproot. In the second year, the plant forms a tall flowerstalk. The stalk is densely covered with small leaves. The showy pale yellow flowers are borne in clusters at the top of the stems. Each flower has 4 petals and 4 green sepals that droop below the petals. As its name implies, the flowers open at dusk.

Edible Parts: Leaves, roots, and shoots.

When to Harvest:
Leaves: Early spring.
Roots: Late fall to early spring.
Shoots: Spring.

How to Harvest:
Leaves: Collect only the young leaves from the first-year plants—those lacking the flowerstalks. The easiest way to identify them is to look for nearby second-year plants that have flowerstalks.
Roots: Again, use only the roots from the first-year plants. The second-year roots are bitter. Dig up the taproot.
Shoots: Collect the young shoots that sprout on second-year plants.

How to Prepare and Cook:

    Leaves: Peel the skin off the leaves with a sharp knife and wash in cold water. Eat the leaves raw in salads or cook them in a small amount of salted water for a pot-herb.

    Roots: Clean and scrape the roots. They can be boiled, roasted, or cooked in soups and stews.

    Shoots: The shoot can be washed and used as a salad green. They have a strong peppery quality and should be mixed with blander greens.

How to Store: Must be used immediately.

RECIPES TO TRY

Candied Evening Primrose Roots

    Clean and scrape 6 evening primrose roots. Boil in 2 changes of salted water until they are tender when pierced with a fork. Peel and slice the roots lengthwise.

Boil together 1 cup brown sugar and ¼ cup water until the mixture becomes a thick syrup. Dip each root in the syrup, season with salt and pepper, and baste with melted butter. Place the roots in a baking dish and bake in a 375° F. oven for 15 to 20 minutes, or until brown. Baste the roots occasionally with syrup. Serves 3 to 6.

Evening Primrose Fritters

    Clean and scrape the 8 roots and boil in two changes of salted water until almost tender. Peel the roots, cool, and cut into slices about ⅛ inch thick.

Sift together 1¼ cups flour and ¼ teaspoon salt. Beat together 1 egg and 1 cup of milk. Add the flour and mix well until batter is smooth.

Dip the sliced roots in the batter and fry in deep fat until golden brown. Drain on a paper towel. Sprinkle with salt, and serve hot. Serves 2 to 4.

Evening Primrose with Cheese

Clean and scrape 8 roots. Boil in two changes of salted water until tender when pierced with a fork. Peel and slice lengthwise. Dip the roots in melted butter and roll them in grated cheese seasoned with salt and pepper. Place on a baking sheet and bake in a 300° F. oven for 15 minutes, or until brown. Serves 2 to 4.

Evening Primrose Omelet

Clean and scrape evening primrose roots and boil in two changes of salted water until almost tender. Peel and dice 2 cups of the roots. To the diced roots, add 2 tablespoons minced onion and ½ teaspoon salt. Sauté the roots and onions in 3 tablespoons of melted butter until tender and brown underneath.

Beat together slightly 5 eggs, 3 tablespoons cream, ½ teaspoon salt, and ¼ teaspoon pepper. Pour the egg mixture over the roots. Cover and cook slowly until the omelet is set, about 8 minutes. Fold and transfer to a hot platter. Serve at once. Serves 4.

American Fried Evening Primrose

Clean and scrape 8 evening primrose roots. Boil the roots in two changes of salted water until almost tender. Let cool, then peel and slice thinly.

Fry 8 slices of bacon in a skillet. Remove the bacon when it is almost crisp. Sauté 3 onions, chopped, in the bacon fat until tender, but not completely browned. Remove the onions and add the sliced roots to the bacon fat. Cook the roots slowly. Turn occasionally so that the roots brown evenly. When the roots are tender, crumble the bacon into the roots and add the onions. Cook until the bacon and onions are heated. Serve hot. Serves 2 to 4.

Gooseberry and Currant

Ribes: And many related species.

Other Common Names: None available.

Picture Reference Numbers: 10, 22

Where to Find: Gooseberry and currant are usually found in moist soil, but some species are found in dry rocky places and others in swamps.

Identifying Characteristics: Gooseberry and currant are small shrubs. The leaves are lobed and veined with coarse teeth around the edges. The flowers are borne on drooping stalks that are attached to the stem along with the leafstalks. The flowers are small with 5 petals and 5 sepals. They vary in color from greenish or yellowish white to purple. The fruits are many seeded berries about ¼ to ⅓ inch in diameter. They have crownlike appendages at the base made of 5 shriveled segments. They vary in color from black to purple, red, or yellow. Gooseberry usually has thorny stems and fine spines on the fruit. The fruit of the currant is smooth-skinned.

Edible Parts: Fruit.

When to Harvest: Fruit: Summer.

How to Harvest: For some reason ripe gooseberries are difficult to find, but they are still good when green.

How to Prepare and Cook: The berries from some of the species are sweet enough to eat fresh; others are sour and better when cooked and sugar is added as in pies, jams, jellies, and wine.

How to Store: The berries can be preserved by drying. To dry in the sun, place washed berries on a screen or stretched cloth in direct sunlight. Cover them with cheesecloth to keep off the flies. Turn occasionally and bring them indoors at night. The berries should be dry in several days. To dry them in the oven, place them on trays and put in the oven under low heat—about 175° F. Store dried fruit in glass jars. To use the dried fruit for making jelly and sauce, add a little hot water.

Additional Information: Gooseberries and currants provide vitamins A, C, and B, and calcium, phosphorous, and iron.

RECIPES TO TRY

Green Gooseberry Pie
Wash 3 cups of green gooseberries. Add the fruit to a mixture of 2 tablespoons flour, 1½ cups sugar, ¼ teaspoon salt, 3 tablespoons of water, and 1 teaspoon of vanilla. Pour into a *baked* 9-inch pie shell. Dot with butter and top with strips of pie dough in a lattice design. Bake in a 450° F. oven for 15 minutes. Lower the heat to 350° F. and bake for another 15 to 20 minutes.

Gooseberry Catsup

Clean and stem 4 pounds of gooseberries in a small amount of water. Add 4 cups of sugar, 2 cups of cider vinegar, 1 tablespoon of cloves, 1 tablespoon cinnamon, 1 tablespoon allspice, 1 tablespoon celery salt, and ¼ teaspoon of cayenne pepper. Simmer the mixture for about 2 hours, or until it thickens to the consistency of tomato catsup. Pour into sterilized jars and seal. Serve with poultry or meat. Yields approximately 3 pints.

Currant Jelly

Cook 1 quart washed currant berries in a small amount of water, mashing the fruit as it cooks. Strain the juice through a jelly bag overnight. Next day, bring 4 cups of the juice to a boil and add 5½ cups of sugar. Heat just enough to dissolve the sugar. Pour into sterilized jars and seal. Yields approximately 3½ pints.

Spiced Gooseberries

Wash and stem 5 pounds of green gooseberries. Boil together 4 pounds of sugar, 1 pint cider vinegar, 1 tablespoon cinnamon, ½ tablespoon allspice, and ½ tablespoon cloves. Add the berries and boil slowly for 20 minutes. Pour into sterilized jars and seal. Yields 5 pints.

Gooseberry Pudding

Pour ⅓ cup of quick tapioca in 2 cups of boiling water and cook for 15 minutes. Boil 2 cups of washed, green gooseberries with 1 cup of sugar until tender. Add 1 tablespoon of lemon juice to the gooseberries and combine with the tapioca mixture. Chill and serve. Top with whipped cream. Serves 6.

Great Bulrush

Scirpus validus and *Scirpus acutus*

Other Common Names: Tule, matrush, and soft-stem bulrush.

Picture Reference Numbers: 11, 23

Where to Find: Bulrush is found in shallow brackish or fresh water of ponds and marshes.

Identifying Characteristics: Bulrush stands from 3 to 6 feet high. The tall naked stems are light green and pithy with circular cross sections. They are soft and easily compressed. The long, tape-like leaves tightly wrap around the stem over much or all of its length to form a sheath. The flowers occur in spikelike clusters just below the tip of the stem. They are either solitary or in groups that hang from short branching stems.

The fruit is tiny, hard, and nearly flat. It is surrounded by 6 bristles attached to the bottom of the fruit and extending slightly above the top.

The roots run parallel to the surface of the ground. They are reddish, stout, and scaly.

Edible Parts: Pollen, seeds, roots, shoots.

When to Harvest:
Pollen: Summer.

Seeds: Fall to winter.
Roots: Fall to early spring.
Shoots: Fall to spring.

How to Harvest:
Pollen: Collect the pollen from the flower spikes.
Seeds: Gather the seeds from the flower spikes (after flowering).
Roots: Dig up the roots.
Shoots: In the fall, dig up and follow the roots to the tips that form next year's shoots. In the spring, pull up young shoots from the roots.

How to Prepare and Cook:
Pollen: The pollen is used like flour.
Seeds: The seeds can be ground and prepared as mush or parched and eaten like nuts.
Roots: Peel off the root hairs and outer rind. Roast for 2 to 3 hours and serve like potatoes or cut into pieces and add to soup and stews.
The younger roots are especially high in natural sugar. A syrup can be made from them by brushing the roots, putting them in a pot of water, and boiling down the liquid for a long time until the desired thickness is reached. Pour off the starchy residue from the syrup.
Shoots: The young shoot is very crisp and tender. It can be eaten raw to relieve thirst and provide sugar, or boiled and added to stews.

How to Store: A good, sweet-tasting flour can be made from the dried roots. After the roots are dried by slow oven-roasting, pound and sift out the fibers. You can also get a flour by boiling the roots into a gruel and removing the fibers. Dry the gruel to a white powder and use for pancakes and breads. The gruel can also be used in the wet state.

Additional Information: The root stock of great bulrush is rich in starch and sugar.

RECIPES TO TRY

Creamed Bulrush and Shrimp

Rinse 1 pound of great bulrush shoots. Steam in a small amount of salted water. Drain and chop finely.

Melt 3 tablespoons butter and blend in 2 to 2½ table-spoons flour. Slowly stir in 1½ cups hot milk. Continue stirring over medium heat with a wire whisk until the mixture is smooth and bubbling. Add 2 cups of chopped bulrush and 1 cup or more of boiled shrimp. Season with salt and pepper to taste. Pour into a greased baking dish. Sprinkle the top with bread crumbs and dot with butter. Bake in a 350° F. oven until browned on top, approximately 30 minutes. Serves 6.

Bulrush Goulash

Cut 2 pounds of round steak into 1-inch cubes. Sauté 1 cup chopped onion in 4 tablespoons butter. Season with 1 teaspoon salt and 1 teaspoon paprika. Brown the meat in the fat and add 1 cup tomato juice. Let simmer for 1 hour. Add 6 to 8 bulrush shoots, washed and sliced. Let simmer for another 30 minutes or until tender. Add more tomato juice if necessary. Serves 4 to 6.

Green Amaranth
Amaranthus retroflexus

Other Common Names: Redroot, pigweed, rough-weed, wild beet.

Picture Reference Numbers: 12, 13, 24

Where to Find: Green amaranth grows as weeds in gardens, cultivated soil, and waste areas.

Identifying characteristics: Green amaranth grows to a height of 3 to 6 feet. It has a stout, hairy stem with few, if any branchings. The greenish flowers, appearing late in summer, are borne at the top of the stem in long, pinnacled spikes. In the fall, the flowers mature to shiny, black seeds. The leaves have a rough surface with wavy margins. The root is bright red.

Edible Parts: Leaves and seeds.

When to Harvest:
  Leaves: Spring to fall.
  Seeds: Fall.

How to Harvest:
  Leaves: Collect young leaves from plants that have not yet flowered. They can be found at the right stage for eating throughout the spring-to-fall growing season.

Seeds: Collect the seeds in the fall when the spikes first become dry. Gather the entire spike and free the seeds by rubbing it between your hands over a container. Winnow out by pouring the seeds from one container to another outdoors and letting the wind blow away the trash.

How to Prepare and Cook:
Leaves: Wash leaves and boil in a small amount of salted water until tender, about 6 minutes. The leaves have a very mild flavor and can be mixed with stronger-tasting greens to tone down their flavor.
Seeds: Grind the seeds between two rocks, with a mortar and pestle, in a kitchen blender, or in a hand flour mill. The seeds make a dark flour used for pancakes and muffins. The somewhat musty flavor is improved when mixed with wheat flour or cornmeal.

How to Store: Green amaranth leaves can be dried on racks in a warm well-ventilated room or in a low oven. Store the dried leaves in glass jars.

Additional Information: Green amaranth leaves are rich in calcium, phosphorous, iron, potassium, and vitamins A, C, and B.

RECIPES TO TRY

Green Amaranth au Gratin
Wash 1 quart green amaranth leaves and steam in a small amount of salted water until tender, about 6 minutes. Drain. Line a shallow pan with the greens and season with salt and pepper. Sprinkle with grated cheese and

14. ARROWHEAD *Sagittaria*

15. BLACK CHERRY *Prunus serotina*

16. BLUE-BERRIED ELDER *Sambucus canadensis—Sambucus melanocarpa*

17. CATTAIL *Typhia latifolia*

18. CHUFA *Cyperus esculentus*

19. DANDELION *Taraxacum offincinale*

20. DOCK *Rumex crispus*

21. EVENING PRIMROSE *Oenothera biennis*

22. GOOSEBERRY *Ribes*

23. GREAT BULRUSH *Scirpus validus and Scirpus acutus*

24. GREEN AMARANTH *Amaranthus retroflexus*

25. HAWTHORN *Crataegus*

26. COMMON SUNFLOWER *Helianthus Annuus*

27. LAMB'S-QUARTERS *Chenopodium album*

28. MINT *Mentha piperita*

29. NETTLE *Urtica Dioica*

30. PURSLANE *Portulaca oleracea*

31. SALSIFY *Tragopogon porrifolius*

32. SHEEP SORREL *Rumex acetosella*

33. SHEPHERD'S-PURSE *Capsella bursa-pastoris*

34. THISTLE *Cirsium vulgare*

35. WILD GRAPE *Vitis*

36. WILD ROSE *Rosa*

37. YELLOW POND LILY *Nuphar advena*

pour 2 or 3 tablespoons cream over all. Broil until the cheese is melted. Serves 4.

Green Amaranth Noodles
Steam green amaranth leaves in a small amount of salted water until tender. Drain and purée in a blender.
Combine ¼ cup puréed leaves with 1 beaten egg and ¼ teaspoon salt. Gradually stir in 2 cups flour and knead until smooth. Place in a greased dish and leave covered for 25 or 30 minutes. On lightly floured cloths, roll the dough into paper thin sheets and let sit until almost dry. Before the dough hardens, cut into thin strips. Separate the strips and allow them to dry thoroughly. Store in glass jars.

Hawthorn

Crataegus: And many related species.

Other Common Names: Haws, thorn apples, red haws

Picture Reference Number: 25

Where to Find: The habitat of hawthorn is extremely varied. It can be found in both wet and dry soil and rocky or rich woods and fields. It is extremely abundant in the limestone areas along the borders of the Appalachian Mountains.

Identifying Characteristics: The size of hawthorn varies from shrubs to small trees of up to 25 feet high. All the species have fierce thorns from 1 to 5 inches long on the smaller branches. The branches are crooked and irregular, and the leaves have serrated edges. The five-petaled flowers, which bloom in the spring, are usually white but in some species, they are red or pink. The fruit is generally red, but some species do produce yellow, blue, or black fruit. The fruit look like tiny apples, each containing from one to five hard nutlets.

Edible Parts: Fruit.

When to Harvest: Fruit: early fall.

How to Harvest: Pick the fruit when it is ripe, usually bright red. The quality of the fruit varies greatly among species, so you should try fruit from different trees.

How to Prepare and Cook: Although even the best of hawthorn fruit is not very palatable when eaten raw, it makes excellent jams and jellies. There is enough natural pectin in the underripe fruit to jell without using a commercial product; but for ripe fruit, it must be added. To make a simple syrup from the haws, put the washed fruit in a saucepan, add a little water and boil to bring out the juice. Strain out the juice, add sugar and boil for another few minutes. The flavor of hawthorns is on the bland side, so you might want to add some almond extract and lemon juice. Use the syrup for a topping on pancakes, etc., or for a base to make jelly.

How to Store: The fruit can be dried in the sun or oven. To dry outdoors, place the washed fruit on a screen or stretched cloth in direct sunlight. Cover with cheesecloth to keep off the flies. Turn the fruit occasionally and bring inside at night. It usually takes several days. To dry in the oven, place on trays and put in a low oven—about 175° F. Store the dried fruit in glass jars.

The dried fruit can be used to make pemmican, a trail food that won't spoil, invented by the Indians. Make patties from the dried fruit mixed with dried meat and fat. The pemmican can be eaten raw, boiled, or fried.

RECIPE TO TRY

Hawthorn Jelly

Extract the juice by boiling several pounds of ripe, washed fruit in 3 or 4 cups of water. Mash the fruit while it is cooking, then strain the juice through a jelly bag. To 4 cups of juice, add 1 (1¾-ounce) package of commercial pectin, the strained juice of two lemons, and ½ teaspoon of almond extract. Bring to a boil, add 5½ cups of sugar, and bring back to a boil. Pour into sterilized jars and seal. Yields 3½ pints.

Jerusalem Artichoke and Common Sunflower
Helianthus tuberosus—Helianthus annuus

Other Common Names: None available.

Picture Reference Numbers: 26, 38, 39

Where to Find: Common sunflowers are found in open fields, especially abundant in western prairies. The Jerusalem artichoke grows in dense clumps in the wilds.

51

Identifying Characteristics: Sunflowers grow to a height of 3 to 6 feet. The most prominent feature of this plant is the large flower head which is composed of a multitude of small, dark brown or purple flowers that make up the center disk and are surrounded by bright yellow ray petals. The disk flowers produce quantities of small seed enclosed by white spotted, blackish brown shells. The oval leaves are rough and toothed. The stalks are fibrous and often are pithy with silky hairs.

The Jerusalem artichoke is similar to the sunflower. However, it grows taller, is more slender and branches more often. It, too, is made up of many flower heads, but these are smaller and don't produce as many edible seeds as those of the common sunflower. The roots of the Jerusalem artichoke are large and tuberous.

Edible Parts: Seeds and tubers.

When to Harvest:
  Seeds: Late summer or early fall.
  Tubers: Fall through spring.

How to Harvest:
  Seeds: Gather the seeds from the common sunflower. The easiest way is to collect the entire flower head and allow it to dry in the sun. The seeds will then shake out easily.
  Tubers: Dig up the tuberous roots of the Jerusalem artichoke.

How to Prepare and Cook:
  Seeds: The seeds need to be hulled before eating. An easy way to do this is crush them and drop them in water. The meat of the seeds will sink to the bottom

while the shells rise to the surface. Skim off the shells—but save. Dry the meats in a slow oven. Roasted, the meats can be eaten like nuts or used as a substitute for nuts in cookies, etc. Hulled meats can also be ground into a flour with a buckwheat taste.

The shells can be roasted, ground, and brewed as a coffee substitute.

A highly nourishing oil can be rendered from the hulled seeds by boiling them in water and skimming the oil off the top after it has cooled.

Tubers: The tubers are shaped like sweet potatoes and have a slightly sweet taste. They can be cooked in the same manner as potatoes—roasted, fried, or boiled. They can also be eaten raw or partially cooked and pickled.

How to Store: The tubers can be stored in a dry cool place and they will keep about as long as potatoes stored in this manner.

Additional Information:

Seeds: Sunflower seeds are 52 per cent protein and 27 per cent carbohydrates. They provide calcium, phosphorous, thiamin, niacin, and riboflavin.

Tubers: The tubers of the Jerusalem artichoke are said to be more nutritious than potatoes.

RECIPES TO TRY

Jerusalem Artichokes and Cream Sauce
Wash and scrape 1½ pounds of Jerusalem artichokes and drop them into salted, boiling water. Cook them until tender. Drain them just as soon as they are tender.

To prepare the white sauce, melt 2 tablespoons of butter over low heat and blend in 2 tablespoons of flour. Slowly stir in 1 cup of hot milk or cream. Season with salt and pepper. Bring to a boil and pour over cooked Jerusalem artichokes. Serve hot. Serves 6 to 8 or more.

Jerusalem Artichokes with White Wine

Wash and scrape 1½ pounds of Jerusalem artichokes and drop them into salted, boiling water. Cook until tender. Drain immediately.

Melt 2 tablespoons of butter over low heat and add 1 teaspoon of white wine, a few drops of Tabasco sauce, and some chopped parsley. Pour over the cooked Jerusalem artichokes and serve. Serves 6 to 8.

Jerusalem Artichoke Salad

Scrape and clean the tubers, and drop into salted, boiling water. Cook until tender. Drain immediately.

For each 4 cups of sliced tubers, add 1 onion, chopped, 1 cup of chopped celery, 1 sliced cucumber, 1 sliced hard-cooked egg, 1 cup of mayonnaise, and ½ teaspoon of salt. Sprinkle with pepper and paprika and serve cold. Four cups serves 6 to 12.

RECIPES TO TRY

Orange Sunflower Bread

Cream 2 tablespoons of butter with ¾ cup of sugar. Add 1 egg. Stir in 1 cup milk, ¾ cup orange juice, and 4 teaspoons grated orange rind.

Sift together 4 cups flour, 4 teaspoons baking powder, and 1 teaspoon salt. Blend the flour into the liquid mixture. Add 1 cup of coarsely ground sunflower seeds.

Pour into a well-greased loaf pan and let it stand for 15 minutes. Bake in a 350° F. oven for 1 hour, or until a toothpick inserted in the center comes out clean.

Sunflower Muffins

Sift together 2 cups of flour, ½ teaspoon salt, and 4 teaspoons baking powder. In another bowl, blend together 1 cup milk, 1 egg, 2 tablespoons sugar, and 3 tablespoons melted butter. Stir in the flour mixture just until the flour is moistened. The batter should be lumpy. Fold in ½ cup of coarsely ground sunflower seeds. Pour into a well-greased muffin tin and bake at 450° F. for 15 to 20 minutes.

Lamb's-quarters

Chenopodium album

Other Common Names: Pigweed, goosefoot, wild spinach.

Picture Reference Numbers: 27, 40

Where to Find: Lamb's-quarters is found in rich soil of cultivated fields and waste areas.

Identifying Characteristics: Lamb's-quarters is an erect, multibranched plant that stands 8 to 48 inches high. The leaves are coated with a slightly waxy, white powder that is most prominent on the underside. Shaped like goosefeet, the leaves are pale green in color and are 1 to 4 inches long and grow at the end of long leafstalks. The older plants bear tiny green flowers on small spikes. After flowering the spikes are covered with small, dull black seeds.

Edible Parts: Entire young plant, leaves, and seeds.

When to Harvest:
  Entire plant: Spring through winter.
  Leaves: Spring and summer.
  Seeds: Fall to winter.

How to Harvest:
  Entire Plant: Pick the young plant, those up to 1 foot tall in its entirety. Young plants can be found at the right stage for eating throughout the growing season. New shoots in older plants are also tender.
  Leaves: Collect the leaves from young plants or the young leaves found at the top of older plants.
  Seeds: The plant produces seeds in great abundance. To collect them, hold a pail under the branches and pull them off. Winnow out the trash by pouring the seeds from one container to another in a breeze. The wind will blow away the trash.

How to Prepare and Cook:
  Entire Plant: The entire plant or the new shoots, washed and shredded, make a nice crisp salad. They can also be cooked as a potherb. Steam for several minutes in a small amount of salted water.
  Leaves: The leaves can be used fresh as a salad green or cooked like spinach for a good potherb. They are not at all bitter, so changing the cooking water is unnecessary.
  Seeds: The seeds make a good seasoning. Added to bread they give bread a pumpernickel-like taste. They

also make a good black flour which is good for pancakes and muffins. The seeds should be completely dried before grinding. They are somewhat difficult to grind. To facilitate this process, boil the seeds first in a little water to soften them. Mash the softened seeds and allow them to dry before grinding.

How to Store: Lamb's-quarters greens can be stored by freezing. Blanch the greens by dipping them in boiling water; pack and freeze.

Additional Information: Lamb's-quarters greens are very rich in vitamins A and C and are a good source of iron, calcium, and potassium.

RECIPES TO TRY

Sweet and Sour Lamb's-quarters

Wash 1½ pounds of lamb's-quarters leaves and shred finely. Fry 4 strips of bacon until crisp. Remove the bacon and sauté the lamb's-quarters in the fat for 8–10 minutes. Add 1 onion, finely chopped, and continue cooking until onion is slightly browned. Add 1 tart apple, diced, and pour in 2 cups boiling water. Let mixture simmer until apples are tender. Sprinkle with 2 tablespoons flour, 4 tablespoons brown sugar, 2 tablespoons vinegar, and let simmer for 5 to 10 minutes more. Crumble bacon over top of mixture and serve hot. Serves 6 to 8.

Lamb's-quarters Cheese Balls

In a small amount of salted water, cook 1½ pounds

lamb's-quarters leaves until tender. Drain 1 cup of the cooked leaves well and chop finely. Add 2 beaten eggs, 1½ cups dry bread crumbs, ½ cup grated cheese, 2 tablespoons finely chopped onion, 1 tablespoon lemon juice, and 1 teaspoon salt. Shape the mixture into small balls and fry in deep fat until brown and crisp. Drain on paper towels. Serves 6 to 8.

Lamb's-quarters Ring

Cook 3 pounds lamb's-quarters in salted water until tender. Drain well. Chop finely.

In a skillet, melt 2 tablespoons butter and add 2 tablespoons flour, stirring with a wire whisk. Add ½ cup milk and stir until smooth and thick. Remove from heat and stir in 3 well-beaten egg yolks. Add the lamb's-quarters and season with salt, pepper, and a little nutmeg. Cool and add 3 stiffly beaten egg whites. Place in a well-greased ring and set in a pan half filled with hot water. Place in a 350° F. oven and bake for 30 minutes or until set. Serves 6.

Mint

Mentha piperita, Mentha spicata

Other Common Names: Peppermint, spearmint.

Picture Reference Numbers: 28, 41

Where to Find: Mint is found in moist soil of fields, meadows, roadside ditches, and stream banks.

Identifying Characteristics: Mint is most easily identified by its characteristic smell. Spearmint leaves are lance-shaped and attach directly to the stem. The blades taper to a sharp point and have unevenly serrated edges. The flowers, appearing in dense clusters at the top of the plant, vary in color from purple to white. Peppermint leaves have short leafstalks. The leaves are narrower than those of the spearmint plant and have evenly serrated edges. The flowers are purple and in loose spikes. The major difference between the two species is the flavor. Peppermint is more pungent and menthol tasting than spearmint.

Edible Parts: Leaves.

When to Harvest: Leaves: Spring and summer.

How to Harvest: Simply pick the leaves off the stem. Quality varies with each plant, so sample the leaves from different plants.

How to Prepare and Cook: Mint leaves are excellent fresh when mixed with other greens in a salad, or steamed in a small amount of salted water and eaten as a cooked vegetable. They, in addition, are used as a flavoring for jellies and sauces and as a seasoning for certain meats. To make mint tea, add to 2 cups boiling water 1 cup chopped leaves. Steep for 5 minutes and strain.

How to Store: Mint leaves keep their flavor when dried and can be stored for a long time in glass jars. Dry the leaves on trays in a slow oven.

Additional Information: Mint leaves provide vitamins A, C, D, E, and K as well as calcium, iron, and potassium.

RECIPES TO TRY

Candied Mint Leaves

Wash the mint leaves and remove the stems. Boil 4 cups of sugar with 2 cups of water until the consistency is that of a very thick syrup. Roll the mint leaves in the syrup. Dry them in a very slow oven, sprinkling occasionally with granulated sugar. The candied mint leaves can be used to decorate candies or cakes, or as a garnish for fruit salads and cocktails.

Mint Salad Dressing

Heat ½ cup vinegar, 2 tablespoons sugar, ¼ teaspoon salt, and a little cayenne pepper in a saucepan. Pour hot mixture over 2 tablespoons of washed, chopped mint leaves and chill.

Mint Butter

Combine 1 tablespoon lemon juice and ¼ teaspoon curry powder with ¼ cup soft butter. Add ¼ cup finely chopped mint leaves. Serve with lamb.

Mint Sauce

Heat 3 tablespoons water with 1½ tablespoons powdered sugar until the sugar dissolves. Cool the syrup and add ⅓ cup finely chopped mint leaves and ½ cup vinegar. Serve with roast lamb.

Mint Jelly

Wipe, quarter, and remove the stems from ½ peck of

tart apples. Put them in a kettle and add enough cold water to barely cover the tops of the apples. Cook apples slowly until they are soft. Mash the apples and drain in a jelly bag overnight.

Next day, boil the apple juice for 5 minutes. Add 1 cup of sugar for each cup of juice. Bring to a boil and let boil for 2 minutes. Add ½ cup of fresh mint leaves and let juice continue to boil until it jells. Then, add 2 tablespoons of lemon juice and some green food coloring. Strain into sterilized jars and seal. Each cup of juice will yield about 1 pint of jelly.

Slender Nettle and Stinging Nettle
Urtica gracilis—Urtica dioica

Other Common Names: None available.

Picture Reference Numbers: 29, 42

Where to Find: Nettle is found in the moist soil of waste places, stream valleys, and rich woods.

Identifying Characteristics: Nettle grows as high as 7 feet, but is usually between 2 and 4 feet high. The leaves are dark green, lighter on the underside, sharply toothed, and often heart-shaped. The leaves, stalks, and stems are covered with hollow, stinging hairs and give off a distinctive odor. The flower cluster is much branched with small greenish flowers.

Edible Parts: Leaves and stems.

When to Harvest:
  Leaves: Spring and summer.
  Stems: Spring and summer.

How to Harvest: In the spring, pick the young leaves and stems. Later in the summer, the newly formed top leaves are also tender enough to eat. *Caution:* The stinging hairs will irritate the skin, so always use protective gloves while gathering nettle. The cooking process neutralizes the toxin and renders the stinging hairs harmless. If you should get "stung" by nettle you can relieve the affected area by rubbing it with the juicy leaves of dock. Dock is usually found growing near nettle.

How to Prepare and Cook: Wash the greens by stirring them in cold water with a long spoon. Remove with tongs and steam for several minutes in a tightly covered pot containing a small amount of salted water. Serve hot with salt and butter.

How to Store: Dry the nettle greens by tying them together and hanging them close to the ceiling in a dry, warm, well-ventilated room, away from direct sunlight. Or, put them on trays in a very slow oven. Store the dried leaves in glass jars in a dark place. The dried leaves can be used to make a very good green tea. Steep the leaves for several minutes in hot water, strain, and sweeten to taste.

Additional Information: Nettle greens are rich in vitamin C, phosphorous, and iron. They also provide vitamin A, calcium, potassium, sodium, and sulphur.

RECIPES TO TRY

Nettle Beer

Boil 2 pounds of washed nettle tops in 1 gallon of water for 15 minutes. In a crock, mix together 2 sliced lemons (rind and all), 2 tablespoons cream of tartar, and 1 pound of sugar. Pour hot water and nettle tops over the mixture in the crock. Let cool to lukewarm and stir in 2 tablespoons brewer's yeast. Bottle and cap tightly. The "beer" will be ready to taste in a few days. When the taste is right, it's ready to drink.

Nettle Soup

Steam 2 pounds of washed nettle leaves for a few minutes. Drain, chop finely, and set aside.

To make the soup base, melt 5 tablespoons of butter and add 4 tablespoons of flour, stirring constantly. Cook for 1 minute, then add 4 cups of chicken or beef stock and stir over low heat until smooth and creamy.

In a small bowl, blend 2 egg yolks and 1 cup of light cream together. Add ½ cup of the soup base and stir with a wire whisk. Pour this egg mixture into the rest of the soup base and blend well. Add the chopped nettle leaves and heat, but do not boil. Season with salt and pepper. Just before serving, top with a pat of butter. Serves 4 to 8.

Nettle Balls

Steam 2 cups of fresh nettle greens in a little salted water. Drain the greens and chop. Mix the chopped greens with 2 tablespoons of butter, 2 tablespoons of grated cheese, 1 tablespoon prepared mustard, and 1 small onion, chopped. Add 1 cup of dry bread crumbs and season with salt and pepper.

When the bread crumbs are moist, form the mixture into small balls. Lightly beat 1 egg with a little cold water. Dip each ball into the egg mixture and then roll in more bread crumbs. Fry the balls in deep fat for 2 to 4 minutes, or until golden brown. Serves 4 to 8.

Purslane

Portulaca oleracea

Other Common Names: Pusley.

Picture Reference Numbers: 30, 43

Where to Find: Purslane is found in fertile sandy soil of old gardens, cultivated fields, and waste areas.

Identifying Characteristics: Purslane is a low plant, spreading over large areas close to the ground. The smooth stems are reddish green to purple in color, and branch frequently. The reddish green leaves, scattered along the stems, are ½ to 2 inches in length, triangular or rounded in shape. Small, yellow, five-petaled flowers are borne at the point where the stems fork. They bloom only in bright sunshine, usually in the morning, and wilt within a few hours. The plant produces many small black seeds, crowded into pods. The pods have a cap at the top that breaks open at maturity.

Edible Parts: Stems and leaves; seeds.

When to Harvest:
Stems and Leaves: Summer and early fall.
Seeds: Late summer.

How to Harvest:
Stems and Leaves: Pick the top leaves and tender tips of the stem.
Seeds: Collect the seeds by pulling up the entire plant and allowing it to dry. In drying, the plant will use up its stored water to ripen all the seed pods at one time. Once dried, spread the plant on a cloth and walk over it to free the seeds from the pods. Remove the trash and winnow out by pouring the seeds from one container to another in a gentle breeze. A gentle wind will blow the small trash away and allow the seeds to fall into the container.

How to Prepare and Cook:
Stems and Leaves: The leaves and stems of purslane are juicy, slightly sour, and thirst-quenching; which makes them good for a trail nibble or salad green. Purslane also makes a very good potherb. Wash the leaves and stems and steam these in a small amount of salted water. Serve with butter and season with salt. They lose very little bulk in cooking, and act as a thickener when added to soups or stews.
Like okra, purslane has a mucilaginous quality that some people don't like. This can be counteracted by rolling the washed tips in flour, dipping into a beaten egg, rolling in bread crumbs and frying in deep fat until golden brown.
Seeds: The seeds can be ground in a blender or hand flour mill to produce flour, which is good alone, or mixed with wheat flour.

65

How to Store: Purslane can be stored several ways. To freeze, blanch the washed tips by quickly dipping them in boiling water, pack in jars and freeze. To dry, tie the stems together and hang near the ceiling in a dry, well-ventilated room. Keep away from direct sunlight. After a few days when they are dry and crumbly, store in glass jars. Use the dried herb when making soups and stews. Purslane stems make an excellent pickle (refer to recipes).

Additional Information: Purslane is a very rich source of iron, and also provides calcium, phosphorous, and vitamins A and C.

RECIPES TO TRY

Pickled Purslane
Wash 4 quarts of purslane tips and place in a crock. Mix together 2 cups salt, 4 cups sugar, 1 cup ground mustard, and 4 quarts of vinegar. Pour mixture over purslane tips and cover with a weighted-down plate. Leave covered for several weeks.

Purslane and Bacon
Fry 6 strips of bacon, chopped in small pieces, until crisp. Add ½ cup vinegar, ½ cup water, 3 teaspoons brown sugar, and 1 quart washed purslane tips; season with salt and pepper. Stir until well coated and serve hot, topped with sliced hard-cooked eggs. Serves 6.

Purslane Casserole
Wash 1 pound of purslane leaves and simmer in salted water for 10 minutes. Drain and chop finely.

Fry 6 slices of bacon until crisp. Remove the bacon and
sauté 1 onion, finely chopped, in the fat.

Mix the purslane leaves with the crumbled bacon and onion.
Add and mix 1 beaten egg and 2 cups dry bread crumbs.
Pour into baking dish and bake in a 350° F. oven until
the top is browned. Serves 4 to 6.

Salsify and Goatsbeard

Tragopogon porrifolius—Tragopogon pratensis

Other Common Names: Salsify—purple oyster plant and
goatsbeard—yellow salsify.

Picture Reference Number: 31

Where to Find: Salsify and goatsbeard are found in open
areas, fields and roadsides.

Identifying Characteristics: This biennial plant grows to a
height of 1 to 3 feet. In the first year the tape-like leaves
form a rosette on top of the taproot. In the second year,
the plant forms a tall flowerstalk with small leaves that
wrap around at the base. The flowers look like large
dandelion heads. They are yellow in goatsbeard and purple in salsify. When the heads go to seed they become
fluffy like dandelions.

Edible Parts: Leaf crowns and roots.

When to Harvest:
   Leaf Crowns: Spring and summer.
   Roots: Spring to fall.

How to Harvest:
   Leaf Crowns: Cut the root about 3 inches below ground level. The leaf crown includes the base of leaves, the stem and the top of the root.
   Roots: Use only the first-year roots. They are not palatable after the flowerstalk has appeared in the second year.

How to Prepare and Cook:
   Leaf Crowns: Steam or boil in a small amount of water. The leaf crown is very tender and requires little cooking.
   Roots: The roots should be boiled in two changes of water with a pinch of bicarbonate of soda added to the first. For a coffee substitute, roast the roots slowly until dark brown. Grind and brew as coffee.

How to Store:
   Leaf Crowns: Must be used immediately.
   Roots: Grind roasted roots. Store in glass jars as you would ground coffee.

Additional Information:
   Salsify is a source of vitamins A and C, calcium, phosphorous, iron, and potassium.

RECIPES TO TRY

Salsify Roots in Cream Sauce
   Wash and scrape 1 to 2 cups roots. Peel and cut into

½-inch slices and boil in salted water until tender, approximately 20 minutes.

Meanwhile, prepare a white sauce by melting 2 tablespoons of butter in a saucepan over low heat. Remove from heat and whisk in 2 tablespoons of flour. Return to heat until mixture bubbles. Add ⅔ cup of hot milk all at once, and then ⅓ cup gradually. Boil, stirring constantly, until the mixture thickens. Season with salt and pepper and serve hot over the cooked salsify roots. Serves 3 to 6.

Fried Salsify

Wash and scrape 4 roots. Boil in salted water until tender. Drain, cool, and peel the roots. Dip each root in milk and roll in bread crumbs that have been seasoned with salt, pepper, and paprika. Fry in hot fat until golden brown, about 20 minutes. Serves 1.

Candied Fried Salsify

Wash and scrape 1 to 2 cups roots and slice lengthwise. Boil in salted water until tender. Drain, cool, and peel. Roll each piece in a mixture of 2 tablespoons sugar, ¼ teaspoon cinnamon, ¼ teaspoon nutmeg, ½ teaspoon salt, and ¼ teaspoon pepper. Dip in butter, roll in flour, and sprinkle with brown sugar. Fry in hot fat until golden brown, about 20 minutes. Serves 3 to 6.

Baked Salsify

Wash and scrape 2 cups roots. Boil in salted water until tender. Drain and peel the roots, then place in a baking dish and sprinkle with salt and pepper, brown sugar, and nutmeg. Dot generously with butter, and pour in enough light cream to cover the bottom of the dish. Top with bread crumbs and bake in a 400° F. oven until the top is brown. Serves 4 to 6.

Sheep Sorrel
Rumex acetosella

Other Common Names: Field sorrel.

Picture Reference Numbers: 32, 44

Where to Find: Sheep sorrel can be found in sour soil of worn-out fields and waste areas.

Identifying Characteristics: Sheep sorrel is similar to dock, but smaller. It grows to a height of 8 to 12 inches. The pale green leaves have a soft texture and a three-lobed arrowhead shape. The flowers are bright red, borne in dense whorls on branches at the upper end of the stem. The red pigment sometimes colors the leaves also. The seeds look like those of dock, but the three winglike membranes surrounding the seed are only obvious at the top of the seed.

Edible Parts: Leaves.

When to Harvest: Spring and summer.

How to Harvest: Pick the young leaves before the plant has flowered.

How to Prepare and Cook: Sheep sorrel leaves contain a sour thirst-quenching juice that's good for a trail nibble.

70

Fresh leaves are also good mixed with other greens in a salad. For a potherb, steam the leaves in a small amount of salted water. You can also add the leaves to soups and stews as a thickener.

For a lemonade-like drink, steep the leaves in hot water, sweeten, and cool.

How to Store: The leaves can be dried to store. Tie the leaves together and hang close to the ceiling in a dry warm place or dry on trays in a very slow (175° F.) oven. Store dried leaves in glass jars in a dark place. Use the dried leaves for soups and stews and as a seasoning for fish or pot roasts.

Additional Information: Sheep sorrel leaves are a good source of vitamin C.

RECIPES TO TRY

Cream of Sheep Sorrel Soup

Wash and shred ½ pound of sheep sorrel leaves. Cook slowly in 2 cups of water for ½ hour. Drain the leaves, but save the juice. Chop leaves finely.

Melt 2 tablespoons of butter and sauté 1 tablespoon of minced onions in the butter. Blend in 1½ tablespoons of flour with a wire whisk. Add ¼ teaspoon salt and ⅛ teaspoon pepper. Stir in slowly 1 cup of milk and 1 cup of water the sheep sorrel leaves were cooked in. Bring to a boil and add chopped sheep sorrel leaves. Let mixture come to boil again and then remove from heat. Serves 4 to 6.

Sheep Sorrel Meringue Pie

Wash 2 cups of sheep sorrel leaves. Shred the leaves and drop into 1 cup of boiling water. Remove from heat and let steep for about ½ hour. Strain the juice.

Beat 4 egg yolks until very light. Blend together ½ cup of butter and 1 cup of sugar until creamy. Beat in the egg yolks and 4 tablespoons of sheep sorrel juice.

To prepare a piecrust, pour ¼ cup of boiling water over ½ cup of shortening and mix until cool and creamy. Sift together 1½ cups of flour, ½ teaspoon baking powder, and ½ teaspoon salt. Add the flour to shortening. Chill in refrigerator until cold enough to roll. Line the bottom of a 9-inch piepan with the dough. Bake in a 500° F. oven for 10 minutes. Pour in the pie filling and bake in a 325° F. oven until firm, about 30 minutes. Let cool and top with meringue.

For the meringue, beat 4 egg whites with ⅛ teaspoon of salt until stiff. Slowly beat in ½ cup sugar and then ½ teaspoon vanilla. Spread over cooled pie and bake in a 300° F. oven for 15 minutes.

Sheep Sorrel Custard

Clean, wash, and finely chop 1 cup of sheep sorrel leaves. Drop into ¾ cup of boiling water and cook for 5 minutes. Remove from heat and let steep for 1½ to 2 hours, until it is reduced to about 2 tablespoons.

Slightly beat 4 egg yolks and add ¼ cup of sugar and ⅛ teaspoon salt. Slowly stir in 2 cups of scalded milk. Add 2 tablespoons of sheep sorrel juice and place over low heat. Stir constantly. Do not allow it to boil at any

38. The easiest way to gather the edible sunflower seeds is to collect the entire flower head and allow it to dry in the sun.

39. The tubers from the Jerusalem artichoke plant are the main ingredient for a dish similar to, but more nutritious than potato salad.

40. Shaped like goosefeet, lamb's-quarters leaves, picked when young, make a nutritious addition to a mixed greens salad.

41. Peppermint leaves have short leaf-stalks and narrow leaves with evenly serrated edges.

42. Nettle grows as high as 7 feet, but is usually between 2 and 4 feet high.

43. The small leaves and the stems of purslane are tart and juicy and therefore make a thirst-quenching trail nibble.

44. Pick the young sheep sorrel leaves before the plant has borne its tiny whorls of bright red flowers. The tiny leaves can be prepared in many ways.

45. A relative to shepherd's-purse, pennycress is similar, but larger. Seeds from both plants can be used as a pepperlike seasoning.

46. Thistle leaves are very tender and mild-tasting, used as a salad green or cooked vegetable.

47. Wild grape leaves can be used to add
a new twist in flavor to pickling
preparations.

48. Rose hips, the ripe fruit of wild rose
plants, are generally considered the
highest natural source of vitamin C.

49. The yellow pond lily seeds make a
good substitute for popcorn kernels.

time. When it has thickened, strain and cool. Add 1 teaspoon vanilla extract and chill thoroughly. Serves 4 to 8.

Sheep Sorrel Salad Dressing

Clean, wash, and finely chop 1 cup of sheep sorrel leaves. Drop into ¾ cup of boiling water and cook for 5 minutes. Remove from heat and let steep for 1½ to 2 hours, until it is reduced to about 2 tablespoons. Beat together ½ cup sour cream, 2 tablespoons sheep sorrel juice, 1 teaspoon sugar, ⅛ teaspoon salt, and pepper to taste. Chill before serving.

Shepherd's-purse

Capsella bursa-pastoris

Other Common Names: Lady's-purse, pepper and salt, pickpocket, shovelweed.

Picture Reference Numbers: 33, 45

Where to Find: Shepherd's-purse is found in sandy soil of fields, waste areas, and roadsides.

Identifying Characteristics: Shepherd's-purse grows from 4 to 24 inches high. The leaves look much like dandelion leaves. They are smooth, toothed, and form a rosette on the ground. A smooth, single stem grows out of the center of the rosette, sometimes branching toward the top. The stem has small, arrowhead-shaped leaves that lack leafstalks. The tiny flowers are white with four petals and are borne along elongated stalks that attach to the stem. The flowers mature to flat, heart-shaped seed pods that resemble old-fashioned purses.

Edible Parts: Leaves and seeds.

When to Harvest:
   Leaves: Spring and summer.
   Seeds: Fall.

How to Harvest:
   Leaves: Collect the young leaves from plants that have not flowered.
   Seeds: Gather the pods, thoroughly dry them, and then crush to free the seeds. Winnow out by pouring the seeds from one container to another in a breeze, and allowing the wind to blow away the trash.

How to Prepare and Cook:
   Leaves: Wash leaves and use them fresh as a salad green. They have a peppery quality. The leaves can also be cooked as a potherb in a small amount of salted water. They are soft and tender, and require very little cooking.
   Seeds: A flour can be prepared from the seeds by parching and grinding them. But, a much better use for the crushed or ground seeds is as a seasoning which gives a peppery quality to food. A relative to shepherd's-purse, pennycress (*Thlaspi arvense*), is similar, but larger. The seeds of pennycress can be used in the same way as those of shepherd's-purse.

How to Store:
   Leaves: Blanch the leaves by quickly dipping them in

74

boiling water. Package and freeze. Or, dry the leaves in a very slow oven and store in glass jars. Use the dried leaves for soups and stews.

Seeds: Crush or grind the seeds and store in glass jars as you would other seasonings.

Additional Information:

Leaves: Shepherd's-purse leaves provide vitamins C and K, as well as calcium, sodium, and sulphur.

RECIPES TO TRY

Shepherd's-purse Cole Slaw

Shred 1 small cabbage finely. Wash young shepherd's-purse leaves under cold running water and tear in small pieces. Shepherd's-purse tastes like pepper and is used according to personal preference. Start by trying 1 leaf per person.

Beat 1 cup sour cream until smooth. Continue beating and add: 2 tablespoons vinegar, 2 tablespoons lemon juice, 1 tablespoon sugar, 1 teaspoon salt, ¼ teaspoon pepper, 1 teaspoon prepared mustard.

Stir cabbage and shepherd's-purse into dressing. Chill and serve. Serves 4 to 6.

Shepherd's-purse and Sour Cream

Wash 2 cups young shepherd's-purse leaves in cold water and blot dry.

Chop several strips of bacon into small pieces and fry until almost crisp. Add the shepherd's-purse and continue cooking for a few minutes more. Drain on paper towel to absorb excess grease. Stir in a small amount of sour cream and serve. Serves 4 to 6.

Thistle

Cirsium vulgare: And related species.

Other Common Names: Hog thistle, bull thistle.

Picture Reference Numbers: 34, 46

Where to Find: Thistle can be found in clearings, meadows, roadsides, and dry waste areas.

Identifying Characteristics: The most distinguishing characteristic of thistle is the spines found at the tip and edges of the leaves and in some species, on the stem. The leaves have no leafstalks and are usually deeply lobed. The flower heads are found at the top of a tall flowerstalk that grows up to 5 feet. The tubular flowers are usually purple, but may be yellow or white. The flowers mature to seed head with white fuzz.

Edible Parts: Leaves, stems, and roots.

When to Harvest:
   Leaves: Spring to fall.
   Stems: Spring through fall.
   Roots: Spring through fall.

How to Harvest:
   Leaves: Use protective gloves as the spines are sharp and irritate the skin.

76

Stems: Using protective gloves cut the stems.

Roots: Thistle is a biennial. Only first-year roots should be used from plants that have not formed the tall flowerstalk.

How to Prepare and Cook:

Leaves: Remove the spines by cutting around the edges with a scissor. Thistle leaves are very tender and mild-tasting. Wash and use them fresh as a salad green or steam them in a small amount of salted water for a pot-herb.

Stems: The best food comes from the stems. Strip the leaves, peel and cut the stem into short sections. Boil them in salted water for an excellent cooked vegetable.

Roots: Wash, scrape, and eat the roots raw, boiled or roasted.

How to Store: The leaves can be frozen. Blanch the washed leaves by quickly dipping them in boiling water, pack and freeze.

RECIPE TO TRY

Thistle Stuffing

Peel the outer skin from thistle stalks and remove spines from the leaves. Combine ½ cup chopped stalks and ½ cup finely chopped leaves. Add 1 cup bread crumbs, 1 small onion, finely chopped, 3 or 4 slices of crumbled cooked bacon, 2 eggs, beaten, ½ tablespoon grated orange rind, ½ tablespoon grated lemon rind, 1 apple cut into cubes, and 2 tablespoons melted butter. Mix the ingredients well. Thistle stuffing is especially good with wild game.

Wild Grape

Vitis: And other related species.

Other Common Names: None available.

Picture Reference Numbers: 35, 47

Where to Find: Wild grapes are found in fertile soil along streams, beaches, and the edges of woods.

Identifying Characteristics: Wild grapes grow on vines that often climb trees, fences, and so forth. The young vines are spiralled; the older vines are covered with gray, shredding bark. The leaves are wide and lobed. The fruit which occurs in clusters varies in size and may be red, purple, or green in color.
Caution: Make sure the fruit has small seeds. If the fruit contains one flat, crescent-shape seed, it is not the wild grape plant but rather a poisonous plant called moonseed.

Edible Parts: Shoot and vine tips, leaves, fruit.

When to Harvest:
  Shoot and Vine Tips: Spring.
  Leaves: Any time (though spring is best).
  Fruit: Fall.

How to Harvest:
  Shoot and Vine Tips: Gather the young shoots and the tips.

Fruit: Pick the grapes off the vine. The smaller varieties are sometimes easier to gather since they occur in denser clusters, enabling you to pick a whole bunch at one time.

How to Prepare and Cook:

Shoot and Vine Tips: The shoot can be eaten raw in salads, or steamed in a small amount of salted water as a cooked vegetable.

Leaves: Grape leaves are really good when steamed for a few minutes, and then sautéed in hot butter. Another really delicious way to eat grape leaves is to stuff them with other food and steam or bake them (see recipes).

Fruit: The fruit can be eaten raw, cooked, or juiced and used to make jellies, pies, and wine.

How to Store:

Shoot and Vine Tips: The shoots and vine tips make good pickles. One quick, simple method is to pack the shoots in jars, add one teaspoon of prepackaged pickling spices, fill the jars with boiling vinegar, and seal. Store the jars for six weeks before eating.

Leaves: Grape leaves used in pickling act like alum and help keep the pickled plant crisp.

Fruit: If left on the vine, the grapes will dry to raisins and cling to the plant all winter. Or, dry them in the sun and store in glass jars.

RECIPES TO TRY

Wild Grape Jelly

Remove the stems and wash 1½ quarts of wild grapes. Use some that are not quite ripe. Crush the grapes, add

½ cup of water, and boil for about 15 minutes. Strain the juice through a jelly bag. Add 4 cups of sugar to 3½ cups of the strained juice and ¼ cup lemon juice. Bring mixture to a boil, stirring constantly. Add 3 fluid ounces of pectin, then bring to a hard boil, stirring constantly, for 1 minute. Remove from heat and skim off foam. Pour the mixture immediately into sterilized jars and seal. Yields 3 pints.

Wild Grape Preserves

Wash, drain, and remove the stems from 4 pounds of wild grapes. Press the pulp from the skins. Boil the pulp, and cook slowly until the seeds are freed. Put this through a fine sieve and return to the kettle. Add the skins and 4 pounds of sugar. Cook slowly for 30 minutes, stirring occasionally. Pour into sterilized jars and seal. Yields 5 pints.

Chocolate-dipped Wild Grapes

Wash and drain 1 pound of grapes, leaving a small stem on each grape. Melt 4 ounces of bitter chocolate in the top of a double boiler. Let it stand until slightly cool. Dip the stem end of each grape into the melted chocolate down to about ¼ of the top of the grape. Let cool for just 1 minute, then roll the chocolate end in some granulated sugar and place chocolate side down on waxed paper to harden.

Stuffed Wild Grape Leaves, Recipe No. 1

Sauté 2 onions, chopped, in 3 tablespoons olive oil. Add 3 tablespoons of pine nuts and ¼ cup of raisins to the onions in the oil, and sauté until entire mixture is warmed. Add ½ cup cooked brown rice to the onions, raisins, and nuts. Remove from heat.

Gather about 40 grape leaves, picked when they are nearly full size but still light green. Stuff leaves with rice mixture, using a small amount in the center of the large portion of each leaf. Fold stem end up, then fold both sides toward the middle. Finally, fold the tip down to completely enclose the stuffing. Place each stuffed leaf seam-edge down in a steamer. Sprinkle with 1 tablespoon of olive oil and 3 tablespoons cold water. Steam for 1 hour, or cook in a pressure cooker at 15 pounds for 30 minutes. Serve hot or cold.

Stuffed Wild Grape Leaves, Recipe No. 2

Bring 2 cups of water to a boil. Add ½ cup wild rice. Turn heat down, cover and simmer for 20 minutes. Add 1 cup long-grain converted rice, recover, and let simmer for another 20 minutes. Set aside.

If desired, cook 1 pound of hamburger, chopped lamb, venison, or other lean meat. Drain away all oil, grease, or water and set aside.

Sauté 1 medium onion, chopped, in 2 tablespoons vegetable oil or butter until onion pieces just *begin* to turn transparent (only a minute or so). Add 1 tablespoon of sweet basil or pennycress. Then add the meat, if used, onions, 1 teaspoon of salt, ½ teaspoon of pepper to the rice mixture and mix well.

Mix 1 pint of tomato sauce, 1 tablespoon of lime or lemon juice, and ½ cup dry red wine, if desired.

Boil about 3 dozen large wild grape leaves for about 3 minutes in slightly salted water. Remove from water and drain well. Cut stems off each leaf. Place leaves on a flat surface with the upper (smoothest) surface of the leaf

facing *down,* and put about 1 heaping tablespoonful
of rice mixture in the middle of each leaf. After 1 or 2
leaves, you'll get to know what quantity of the rice mixture works best. Fold the sides of each leaf over rice
mixture and, starting at the stem end of the leaf, roll
tightly *with* the midrib of the leaf. The finished roll will
be about three times as long as it is wide.

Place rolls in a shallow pan (or pans) and cover with
tomato sauce mixture. Cover pan(s) and simmer (steam)
on top of stove for 30 minutes. The stuffed leaves are
good hot or *chilled.*

Wild Rose

Rosa: And several other species.

Other Common Names: None available.

Picture Reference Numbers: 36, 48

Where to Find: Wild roses can be found almost anywhere, but especially in gravelly soil and along roadsides.

Identifying Characteristics: Wild roses grow on small
shrubs with thorned, branched stems. The leaves are
dark green and the flowers are pink or rose-colored. Toward late summer, the seed pods, or ripe fruit, begin
to swell and darken to tufted orange or red capsules.
These capsules, called rose hips, cling to the shrubs
throughout winter.

Edible Parts: Petals and rose hips.

When to Harvest:
   Petals: Early summer.
   Rose Hips: Fall through winter.

How to Harvest:
   Petals: Gather the petals from the blossoms.
   Rose Hips: Rose hips are best gathered when bright in color, but can be harvested at any time.

How to Prepare and Cook:
   Petals: Cut off white part at the base of the petal, as this is bitter. The fresh petals can be used in salads, on sandwiches, and in jams.
   Rose Hips: To prepare rose hips, pare off the tufts and cut in half. Remove the seeds, but save them. (See storing tips below.) The fruit can be eaten raw, cooked like fresh fruit, or boiled down to syrup. To make a simple syrup, bring the fruit to a boil in a pot containing a small amount of water; about 1 cup of water per quart of fruit. Continue boiling for about 20 minutes or until juicy. Squeeze the contents of the pot through a jelly bag, and return the juice to the saucepan. Add sugar and boil the two together until mixture thickens, about 5 minutes. The syrup can be stored in a jar in the refrigerator and used as a topping for pancakes, waffles, etc., or as a fruit base for jelly. Do not use aluminum or copper utensils; they lower or destroy vitamin C.

How to Store:
   Petals: Dry the petals on trays in a very slow oven, about 175° F., and store in glass jars. Use the dried petals to

make tea. Cover 2 tablespoons of the petals with boiling water, and steep for five minutes. Strain and sweeten with sugar and honey.

Rose Hips: Rose hips can be stored by drying. Cut the fruit in half and remove the seeds. Place the fruit halves in a slow oven to dry. Partially dried fruit can be eaten alone like raisins, or added to cereal. Completely dried rose hips can be crushed into a powder and stored. Add the highly nutritional powder to flour for baked products. The seeds can also be dried, ground, and added to flour. Both the fruit and the seeds used in this way serve to increase and supplement the nutritional value of different flours.

Additional Information: Rose hips are the highest natural common source of vitamin C, much higher than oranges. They also provide iron, calcium, and phosphorous. The seeds are rich in vitamin E.

RECIPES TO TRY

Rose Petal Jam

Use 1 cup of petals with the white base cut off and 1 cup of rose hips. Put the petals and the rose hips in a blender with 1 cup of water and 1 tablespoon of lemon juice, blending until smooth. Add 2 cups of sugar and continue blending until the sugar has dissolved.

Stir 1 (1¾-ounce) package of commercial pectin into ¾ cup water. Bring to a boil and let boil rapidly for 1 minute, stirring constantly. Pour the mixture into the blender with the rose petal mixture and blend slowly. Pour into sterilized jars and seal. Yields 3 pints.

Candied Rose Hips

Remove the seeds from the hips and boil 1½ cups rose hips with ½ cup sugar and ¼ cup water for 10 minutes. Lift the fruit from the syrup and drain on waxed paper. Dust the hips with sugar and dry in a very slow oven. Store between sheets of waxed paper in a covered metal container. The candied rose hips can be used as nuts or chopped fruit in cookies, fruit squares, and fruit cake.

Rose Hip and Rhubarb Jam

Use slightly underripe rose hips. Cut them in half and remove the seeds. Boil 1 cup rose hips with 1 cup of water, 4 cups diced rhubarb, and ¼ teaspoon salt for 1 minute. Add 2 cups sugar and 1 tablespoon grated lemon rind and boil for another minute. Pour into sterilized jars and seal. Yields 3 pints.

Rose Hip Syrup

Wash rose hips and boil 4 cups hips with 2 cups of water in a covered saucepan for 20 minutes. Strain through a jelly bag to clear the sediment from the mixture. Return the strained juice to the saucepan and add 2 cups of sugar. Boil the juice and sugar for 5 minutes. Pour into jars and refrigerate until ready to use. Syrup will keep indefinitely. Yields about 3 pints.

Yellow Pond Lily

Nuphar advena: And other related species.

Other Common Names: Spatterdock, cow lily, water collard, and yellow water lily.

Picture Reference Numbers: 37, 49

Where to Find: Yellow pond lily can be found in lakes, ponds, pools, swamps, and tidal marshes.

Identifying Characteristics: The glossy leaves of yellow pond lily have broad rounded or elliptical blades that are deeply clefted at the base. They are usually raised several inches above the water surface at the end of a long spongy leafstalk. Immature leaves are found floating or submerged. The leafstalk extends to the bottom of the water rising directly from the top of a thick fleshy root. The flowers are borne singly on long flowerstalks that also rise directly from the root and extend above the water surface. The flowers are spherical cups made of smooth petal-like sepals enclosing many small golden yellow petals. Fully opened flowers reach up to 5 inches in diameter. In the late summer or early fall, the flowers mature into urn-shaped fruits, about 2 inches high and 2 inches across. These fruits, or seed pods, are filled with seeds resembling the size and shape of popcorn kernels.

Edible Parts: Seeds and roots.

When to Harvest:
   Seeds: Late summer or early fall.
   Roots: Fall to early spring.

How to Harvest:
   Seeds: Cut the pods free from the stalk and let dry in the sun. Now the pod can be easily pulled apart for the seeds.
   Roots: In shallow water the roots are easily pulled free from the mud.

How to Prepare and Cook:
   Seeds: The seeds make a good substitute for popcorn. Pop as you would popcorn, adding melted butter and salt. The seeds can also be parched, pounded slightly, then boiled and eaten like rice; or, ground into meal.
   Roots: Wash, scrape, and peel the roots. If the strong taste is disagreeable to you, remove it by boiling them in 2 changes of water. The roots can then be roasted whole or sliced and fried.

How to Store:
   Seeds: Store seeds in glass jars as you would popcorn kernels or any ground meal.
   Roots: Must be used immediately.

RECIPES TO TRY

Yellow Pond Lily Casserole
   Clean, scrape, and peel 6 to 8 medium-sized yellow pond

lily roots. Boil in 2 changes of salted water until tender. Slice the roots and arrange one layer in the bottom of a buttered casserole dish. Sprinkle the layer with brown sugar and dot with butter. Cover with a layer of thinly sliced unpeeled oranges. Repeat the layers until all the roots are used. Combine ¼ cup honey with ½ cup orange juice and pour over the layers. Combine ¼ cup fine dry bread crumbs with 2 tablespoons brown sugar and 1 tablespoon butter, and sprinkle over top layer. Cover and bake in a 350° F. oven for 30 to 40 minutes. Remove the cover during the last 15 minutes of baking time. Serves 3 to 6.

Scalloped Yellow Pond Lily Roots

Clean and peel 6 to 8 medium-sized yellow pond lily roots. Boil in 2 changes of salted water until almost tender.

Cover the bottom of a buttered baking dish with fine dry bread crumbs. Dot with butter and sprinkle with minced parsley. Cover with a layer of sliced roots. Salt and pepper to taste. Repeat the layers until all the roots are used. Pour 1 cup of milk over all and bake in a 300° F. oven for 1 hour. Serves 3 to 6.

Maple Candied Yellow Pond Lily Roots

Clean, scrape, and peel 1 dozen yellow pond lily roots. Boil in 2 changes of salted water until almost tender. Slice the cooked roots and place in a greased baking dish.

Boil together 1 cup maple syrup, 2 tablespoons butter, 2 teaspoons salt, 2 cups apple cider, and 1 cup water. Pour over the sliced roots and bake in a 300° F. oven for 1 hour. Serves 3 to 6.

Yellow Pond Lily Popcorn Balls

Take dried seeds from the yellow pond lily and pop in the same way as you would pop corn.

Combine in a saucepan 2 cups of sugar, 5 tablespoons molasses, 5 tablespoons water, and a pinch of cream of tartar. Boil until the syrup will form a firm ball when dropped into cold water. Remove the syrup from the heat and allow it to cool for a minute or two. Add 2 tablespoons butter and 1 teaspoon vanilla extract. Gently stir in 2 cups of the popped seeds until they are well coated. When cool enough to handle, form into balls.

APPENDIX

HARVESTING CHART

L = late in season
E = early in season

Plant	Spring	Summer	Fall	Winter
Arrowhead			tubers	tubers
Black Cherry & Chokecherry		fruit (L)	fruit (E)	
Blue-berried Elder		blossoms fruit (L)	fruit (E)	
Cattail	spikes shoots roots	pollen stem roots	roots	roots
Chufa	tubers	tubers	tubers	
Dandelion	leaves (E) blossoms leaf crowns roots	blossoms (E) leaf crowns roots	roots	roots
Dock	leaves		seeds	
Evening Primrose	leaves (E) shoots		roots (L)	roots
Gooseberry & Currant		fruit		
Great Bulrush		pollen	seeds shoots roots	shoots roots
Green Amaranth	leaves	leaves	seeds	
Hawthorn			fruit (E)	
Jerusalem Artichoke & Sunflower		seeds (L)	tubers seeds (E)	tubers
Lamb's-quarters	entire young plant leaves	entire young plant leaves	entire young plant seeds	seeds

HARVESTING CHART (continued)

L = late in season
E = early in season

Plant	Spring	Summer	Fall	Winter
Mint	leaves	leaves		
Nettle	leaves stems	leaves stems		
Purslane		seeds (L) leaves stems	seeds (E) leaves (E) stems (E)	
Salsify & Goatsbeard	leaf crowns roots	leaf crowns roots		
Sheep Sorrel	leaves	leaves		
Shepherd's-purse	leaves	leaves	seeds	
Thistle	leaves stems roots	leaves stems roots	leaves stems roots	
Wild Grape	leaves shoots vine tips	leaves fruit (L)	leaves fruit	leaves
Wild Rose		petals (E)	rose hips	rose hips
Yellow Pond Lily		seeds (L)	roots seeds (E)	roots

SAMPLE FOOD VALUES OF SELECTED WILD PLANTS*

Plant		Water	Food Energy	Protein	Fat	Carbohydrates Total	Carbohydrates Fiber	Ash	Calcium
		percentage	calories	grams	grams	grams	grams	grams	milligrams
Blue-berried Elder (raw)	raw	79.8	72	2.6	.5	16.4	7.0	.7	38
Dandelion Greens	cooked	85.6	45	2.7	.7	9.2	1.6	1.8	187
	raw	89.8	33	2.0	.6	6.4	1.3	1.2	140
Dock	cooked	90.9	28	2.1	.3	5.6	.8	1.1	66
		93.6	19	1.6	.2	3.9	.7	.7	55
Gooseberry (raw)		88.9	39	.8	.2	9.7	1.9	.4	18
Great Bulrush (canned, water-packed)		92.5	26	.5	.1	6.6	1.3	.3	12
Green Amaranth (raw)		86.9	36	3.5	.5	6.5	1.3	2.6	267
Jerusalem Artichoke (raw)		79.8	88	2.3	.1	16.7	.8	1.1	14
Lamb's-quarters	raw	84.3	43	4.2	.8	7.3	2.1	3.4	309
	cooked	88.9	32	3.2	.7	5.0	1.8	2.2	258
Purslane (leaves & stems)	raw	92.5	21	1.7	.4	3.8	.9	1.6	103
	cooked	94.7	15	1.2	.3	2.8	.8	1.0	86
Salsify	raw	77.6	13 - 82	2.9	.6	18.0	1.8	.9	47
	cooked	81.0	12 - 70	2.6	.6	15.1	1.8	.7	42
Sheep Sorrel	raw	90.9	28	2.1	.3	5.6	.8	1.1	66
	cooked	93.6	19	1.6	.2	3.9	.7	.7	55
Sunflower Seeds		4.8	560	24.0	47.3	19.9	3.8	4.0	120

Source: COMPOSITION OF FOODS Agricultural Handbook #8. Consumer and Food Economics Research Division. Agricultural Research Service — U. S. Department of Agriculture.

*per 100 grams.

SAMPLE FOOD VALUES OF SELECTED WILD PLANTS* — (continued)

Plant		Phosphorus milligrams	Iron milligrams	Sodium milligrams	Potassium milligrams	Vitamin A international units	Thiamine milligrams	Riboflavin milligrams	Niacin milligrams	Ascorbic Acid milligrams
Blue-berried Elder (raw)		28	1.6	—	300	600	.07	.06	.5	36
Dandelion Greens	raw	66	3.1	76	397	14,000	.19	.26	—	35
	cooked	42	1.8	44	232	11,700	.13	.16	—	18
Dock	raw	41	1.6	5	338	12,900	.09	.22	.5	119
	cooked	26	.9	3	198	10,800	.06	.13	.4	54
Gooseberry (raw)		15	0.5	1	155	290	—	—	—	33
Great Bulrush (canned, water-packed)		10	.3	1	105	200	—	—	—	11
Green Amaranth (raw)		67	3.9	—	411	6,100	.08	.16	1.4	80
Jerusalem Artichoke (raw)		78	3.4	—	—	20	.20	.06	1.3	4
Lamb's-quarters	raw	72	1.2	—	—	11,600	.16	.44	1.2	80
	cooked	45	.7	—	—	9,700	.10	.26	.9	37
Purslane (leaves & stems)	raw	39	3.5	—	—	2,500	.03	.10	.5	25
	cooked	24	1.2	—	—	2,100	.02	.06	.4	12
Salsify	raw	66	1.5	—	380	10	.04	.04	.3	11
	cooked	53	1.3	—	266	10	.03	.04	.2	7
Sheep Sorrel	raw	41	1.6	5	338	12,900	.09	.22	.5	119
	cooked	26	.9	3	198	10,800	.06	.13	.4	54
Sunflower Seeds		837	7.1	30	920	50	1.96	.23	5.4	—

* per 100 grams

BIBLIOGRAPHY

Angier, Bradford. FEASTING FREE ON WILD EDIBLES: Stackpole Books, Harrisburg, Pa., 1972.

Angier, Bradford. GOURMET COOKING FOR FREE: Stackpole Books, Harrisburg, Pa., 1970.

Berglund, Berndt, and Bolsby, Clare E. THE EDIBLE WILD: Charles Scribner's Sons, New York, N.Y., 1971.

Bleything, Dennis. EDIBLE PLANTS IN THE WILDERNESS: 2 volumes; Life Support Technology, Inc., Beaverton, Ore., 1972.

Crowhurst, Adrienne. THE WILD COOKBOOK: Lancer Books, Inc., New York, N.Y., 1972.

Gibbons, Euell. STALKING THE HEALTHFUL HERBS: David McKay Co., New York, N.Y., 1966.

Gibbons, Euell. STALKING THE WILD ASPARAGUS: David McKay Co., New York, N.Y., 1962.

Hall, Alan. THE WILD FOOD TRAILGUIDE: Holt, Rinehart and Winston of Canada, U.S.A., 1973.

Harris, Bea Charles. EAT THE WEEDS: Barre Publishers, Barre, Mass., 1968.

Medsger, Oliver Perry. EDIBLE WILD PLANTS: The Macmillan Co., New York, N.Y., 1966.